Intelligence: A Very Short Introduction

'I can, and shall, recommend this engaging book to anyone,
student or layperson . . . a reasoned and reasonable view of this
interesting and important topic.'
Professor N. J. Mackintosh, Cambridge University

'This book, written by one of the world's leading researchers on
intelligence, provides an ideal introduction to a controversial topic.
Deary . . . tells us in an entertaining and clear way what was done, what
was found, and what it does and does not mean. . . . If you want to know
how we know what we know about intelligence read this book.'
Nat Brody, Wesleyan University

'Professor Deary's short introductory book about human intelligence is
like no other account available. He addresses the big issues that the
experts continue to debate . . . all in an easy-to-digest, balanced style
that meets his aim to put the reader in touch with the scientific
research into this challenging field. This book is first class.'
Ted Nettelbeck, Adelaide University

'succinct and high   /hat is and is
not known abo   iat will be of

VERY SHORT INTRODUCTIONS are for anyone wanting a stimulating and accessible way in to a new subject. They are written by experts, and have been published in more than 25 languages worldwide.

The series began in 1995, and now represents a wide variety of topics in history, philosophy, religion, science, and the humanities. Over the next few years it will grow to a library of around 200 volumes – a Very Short Introduction to everything from ancient Egypt and Indian philosophy to conceptual art and cosmology.

Very Short Introductions available now:

Available soon:

AFRICAN HISTORY
  John Parker and Richard Rathbone
ANCIENT EGYPT   Ian Shaw
THE BRAIN   Michael O'Shea
BUDDHIST ETHICS
  Damien Keown
CHAOS   Leonard Smith
CHRISTIANITY   Linda Woodhead
CITIZENSHIP   Richard Bellamy
CLASSICAL ARCHITECTURE
  Robert Tavernor
CLONING   Arlene Judith Klotzko
CONTEMPORARY ART
  Julian Stallabrass
THE CRUSADES
  Christopher Tyerman
DERRIDA   Simon Glendinning
DESIGN   John Heskett
DINOSAURS   David Norman
DREAMING   J. Allan Hobson
ECONOMICS   Partha Dasgupta
THE END OF THE WORLD
  Bill McGuire
EXISTENTIALISM   Thomas Flynn
THE FIRST WORLD WAR
  Michael Howard
FREE WILL   Thomas Pink
FUNDAMENTALISM
  Malise Ruthven
HABERMAS   Gordon Finlayson

HIEROGLYPHS
  Penelope Wilson
HIROSHIMA   B. R. Tomlinson
HUMAN EVOLUTION
  Bernard Wood
INTERNATIONAL RELATIONS
  Paul Wilkinson
JAZZ   Brian Morton
MANDELA   Tom Lodge
MEDICAL ETHICS
  Tony Hope
THE MIND   Martin Davies
MYTH   Robert Segal
NATIONALISM   Steven Grosby
PERCEPTION   Richard Gregory
PHILOSOPHY OF RELIGION
  Jack Copeland and Diane Proudfoot
PHOTOGRAPHY
  Steve Edwards
THE RAJ   Denis Judd
THE RENAISSANCE
  Jerry Brotton
RENAISSANCE ART
  Geraldine Johnson
SARTRE   Christina Howells
THE SPANISH CIVIL WAR
  Helen Graham
TRAGEDY   Adrian Poole
THE TWENTIETH CENTURY
  Martin Conway

For more information visit our web site
www.oup.co.uk/vsi

Ian J. Deary

INTELLIGENCE

A Very Short Introduction

OXFORD
UNIVERSITY PRESS

Great Clarendon Street, Oxford OX2 6DP

Oxford University Press is a department of the University of Oxford.
It furthers the University's objective of excellence in research, scholarship,
and education by publishing worldwide in

Oxford New York

Auckland Bangkok Buenos Aires Cape Town Chennai
Dar es Salaam Delhi Hong Kong Istanbul Karachi Kolkata
Kuala Lumpur Madrid Melbourne Mexico City Mumbai Nairobi
São Paulo Shanghai Taipei Tokyo Toronto

Oxford is a registered trade mark of Oxford University Press
in the UK and in certain other countries

Published in the United States
by Oxford University Press Inc., New York

© Ian J. Deary 2001

British Library Cataloguing in Publication Data
Data available

Library of Congress Cataloging in Publication Data
Data available

ISBN 978-0-19-289321-5

13 15 17 19 20 18 16 14

Typeset by RefineCatch Ltd, Bungay, Suffolk
Printed in Great Britain by
Ashford Colour Press Ltd, Gosport, Hampshire

Contents

List of illustrations

Preface and acknowledgements

People value their powers of thinking, and most of us are interested in why some people seem to drive a highly tuned Rolls Royce brain while others potter along with a merely serviceable Ford Fiesta. The fact that the broad powers of human intelligence show differences has been recognized since antiquity. Our language is full of words that signify the possession or lack of an efficient brain. Within the academic discipline of psychology there is a subsection of researchers and teachers called 'differential psychologists'. They study the differences between people in intelligence and personality. In this short book, I want to describe what they have discovered about how and why people differ in their thinking powers.

There are many books on human intelligence differences and it needed a good reason to add one to the pile. Beyond the tracts written by academics for their peers and students, two sorts of popular book predominate. On the one hand there are many test-your-IQ-type books that offer an introduction to the field of mental measurement. Depending on how you score on their tests, they will flatter or depress. They act as a sort of do-it-yourself fitness diagnosis for your brain. They are a mostly harmless diversion: probably it's only rather bright people who buy them anyway, and end up rather pleased with the results. On the other hand, there are books which denounce IQ testing as a form of social evil, as a tool used by a social elite to keep the lower orders in their places. Neither of these types of book is satisfactory for understanding the key information about human mental abilities. The former is a quack diagnostic kit and the latter sells a political message that relegates research facts and emphasizes spin.

And it is facts that drive this present book. It is an attempt to cut out the middle man and put you in touch with some actual research data in human intelligence. There is no such thing as a *theory* of human intelligence differences – not in the way that grown-up sciences like physics or chemistry have theories. We don't know enough about the workings of the brain to say why some brains seem to be more efficient than others. However, there are some *hard facts* about human intelligence differences. Just as in other sciences, these hard facts constrain what we can say about the topic: we should not be claiming things that go against or ignore the best evidence in the field. And just as we should expect of a science, we also have to be frank in admitting the faults of each study, especially when the results seem to agree with our own prejudices. The best scientists are their own most severe critics.

The plan of the book is to present a series of diagrams, each of which captures a solid finding about human intelligence differences. Here and there, the diagrams might look quite complicated. The promise is that you will understand them by reading the accompanying text. My efforts have been aimed toward a clear, non-technical, but also uncompromisingly accurate, account of some of the important areas in human intelligence. The sources from which I drew the information are fully documented here, but no one study is without fault and no single study can settle an issue. My opinion, though, is that it is better to know some influential studies and their main results than merely to amass third-hand accounts which sell a point of view by selective reporting.

I've selected 11 sets of research results, 11 datasets, that I think address central questions about human intelligence: not exactly '11 datasets that shook the world', but all are influential in the field. Some of these are remarkable single sets of data that represent huge amounts of effort, luck, and/or ingenuity on the part of the investigator(s). Some of them are collections of studies on a topic that have taken decades to put together and synthesize. There are some descriptions of the work involved in conducting the studies, so that they are not just dry numerical accounts. The datasets address some of the most interesting questions about human intelligence: what forms does it take?; what happens to it as we grow old?; are its origins in our genetic code and the environment's influences?; does it matter in real life?; why is it rising generation after generation?; and do psychologists themselves agree about intelligence?

For each of the datasets I have chosen one or more illustrations that capture some important aspect of the results. Most of these illustrations originally appeared in the research articles reporting the data. Rather than reproduce these sometimes technical diagrams, they are redrawn in a more accessible form.

Really the 11 datasets are just introductions to a field in which many of us are spending our research lives investigating one or more small patches. In order to assist interested readers in following up some specific topics, there are suggestions at the end of each chapter for how you might develop your interest in the given areas and do some further reading. There is also a section at the end of the book offering general ideas on further resources.

Between them, Rosalind Arden and Shelley Cox flattered me into thinking I could write something accessible about human intelligence differences. Linda Gottfredson, Shelley Cox, Tracy Miller, and Alan Bedford made good suggestions on earlier drafts. I thank those whose datasets are the fabric of this short treatment. An author must have an audience in his mind's eye. Mine was focused on my intelligent and incredulous mother, Isobelle.

A word about correlation

This series of Very Short Introduction books, and this particular book on human intelligence, is intended for the general, interested reader. The material aims to be accessible but still intellectually pithy. I have tried to avoid patronizing generalizations in favour of demonstrating what a real research project in this field looks like, and what it can and cannot tell us. My reason for taking this course was that, among popular accounts of intelligence research, one can find diametrically opposed views about the same sets of data. Therefore, I wanted the reader to think about actual findings, not the Chinese whispers issuing from several-times-digested summaries of the research.

The approach adopted here erects one hurdle that I have to clear. The use of statistics is central to research on intelligence. Researchers typically test large numbers of people on a variety of mental tests, and discovering the pattern and significance of the differences between people cannot be done without statistical examination of the data. Some of the key debates in human intelligence are about statistical matters. Further, the statistics we employ in intelligence research are among the more complicated in the discipline of psychology. Now, there was no point in trying to fashion a general book that was replete with statistics: no one would read it. In the end I decided that there was no escaping one type of statistic: *correlation*. This is easy to understand. If you know what correlation is, just skip the rest of this section and move on to Chapter 1. If you don't, read the following non-technical explanation.

Correlation is a way of describing how closely two things relate to each other. It is expressed as a number called a correlation coefficient. The range of values that a correlation coefficient can take is from −1 through 0 to 1.

Take an example. Say that I stop the first 100 adult women I meet in the street and measure their heights and weights. I am curious to know, let's suppose, whether being taller also means being heavier. A correlation coefficient can be calculated according to a formula and it will tell me how strongly the two are related. Imagine that everyone who was taller than someone else was also heavier than them. There would be a perfect association between the two: the correlation would be 1. That's not going to happen. The situation in real life is that we all know some short fat people and some tall thin people. On the whole the taller people are heavier, but there are many exceptions. Therefore, there is a strong trend toward taller people weighing more, but it is not perfect. The correlation is probably around 0.5, a highish positive correlation.

Extend that example. Say I also decided to measure the length of their hair. I am curious to know whether the taller people grow their hair longer. I am almost certain that there is no tendency whatever for tall people to have their hair either longer or shorter than smaller people. My guess is that height would have absolutely no association with hair length at all. If I am correct, the correlation coefficient would be 0. The two things have no tendency to go together.

One more extension to the example. Let's say that in addition to measuring people's heights we ask them to walk a measured distance, say 20 metres. We count the number of steps it takes them. I am curious to know whether there is any association between height and the number of steps it takes to cross this distance. My guess is that taller people would on the whole take fewer strides. The correlation coefficient would probably confirm this; but note that it would find that being taller would go along with a smaller number of steps. So the correlation would be negative; as one value (height) goes up, the other one (steps taken to cover 20 metres) goes down. It might be about −0.4. However, the value is not the important thing here. The point I want to get across is that important, strong correlations can have negative *or* positive values. It's when the value of the correlation is zero that there is no relationship between two things.

A correlation can describe for us whether one thing tends to go up or down with another thing, or whether there is no relation at all between the two.

Next, a word about the sizes of correlations. I mentioned above that height and weight probably had a fairly high correlation, about 0.5 or thereabouts, or maybe more. (In fact, I got the 0.5 value by calculating it from heights and weights of a number of people's data that I happened to have on my computer.) In psychology and other sciences that look at social phenomena, we do not often find correlations beyond about the 0.5 level. There is a convention that correlation coefficients above about 0.5 are called *large* or *strong effects*. Those between about 0.2 and 0.5 are called *medium*, *modest*, or *moderate*. Those below 0.2 are called *small* or *weak*.

Last, a word about the nomenclature I shall use. For variety I shall not always refer to correlations between two things. Sometimes I shall say the 'relation' or the 'relationship' and at other times I shall say the 'association'. When I use these words I am referring to a correlation. And if I qualify any of these terms with the adjectives large, medium, or small, these will refer to the sizes of coefficient mentioned in the previous paragraph.

In much of the material that follows, we shall use the correlation coefficient to describe how strongly intelligence test scores relate to other things. Sometimes I shall be looking at whether one type of intelligence test has a high correlation with another type. Sometimes I shall be asking whether intelligence test scores correlate with anything about our achievements in real life. And sometimes I shall be asking whether anything about our brains and brain functions correlates with intelligence test scores.

It is important to emphasize that correlations describe the relation between two things that we have measured in a *group* of people. Indeed, the larger that group is the more confident we can be that the correlation value is the correct one. So, the value applies across a group that we have measured. But people make the common error of applying the correlation to themselves personally. Let's say we announce that we have tested heights and weights of people and we say that there is a strong correlation, such that taller people tend to be heavier. A short, portly person might well look at themselves and exclaim that we are talking nonsense, that they are living proof that there's no such association. We must recall that in any situation where a correlation is not +1 or −1 (i.e. almost all the time), we shall find exceptions to the association that we have found. The lower the correlation, the more exceptions we shall find as we meet up with individual people.

So, correlations are summaries that tell us about the association between two things in a given sample of people. They don't tell us about individuals. Moreover, they don't necessarily tell us that we shall find the same association in other samples of people. If we find a correlation between two things in adult men we cannot assume that we should find the same correlation in children or in women, for example.

Here is a practical example from the world of intelligence research that makes the point again about groups of people versus individuals.

There's a modest correlation between scores on intelligence tests and job status. The UK government has produced a book in which researchers can grade people's jobs according to a scale. At one end of this scale there are professional jobs, like those of lawyers and doctors, and at the other end there are tasks like manual labouring. As I said, there is a modest correlation between intelligence test scores and job status, perhaps about 0.4 or a bit above that. That tells us something about a group of people: it says that, in general, there will be a tendency for the people with higher intelligence test scores to get more skilled and professional jobs. But, because the correlation is not very strong, it means there will be many exceptions. When we start to look at individual people, we shall find some lower scorers who ended up in professional jobs and higher scorers who are working with their hands. Therefore, correlations – even quite strong ones – do not tell us about individuals: a correlation is a description of a *tendency* in a *group* of people.

And there's another lesson from this. Take the correlation between intelligence and job status. Because that correlation is not especially high, it means that there's a lot more to getting a good job and a high salary than high intelligence. This is what we shall see all along the line: intelligence might have some influence on things, but there is always a lot more to any human story than just intelligence.

To follow this area up . . .

There are good descriptions of correlation, in settings related to intelligence, in the following books.

Cooper, C. (1999). *Individual Differences*. London: Arnold.
Herrnstein, R. J. & C. Murray (1994). *The Bell Curve*. New York: Free Press.

The following is a good and accessible introduction if you want to read more about the conceptual and statistical issues related to measuring intelligence ('psychometrics') and other aspects of the human psyche.

Kline, P. (2000, 2nd edn). *Handbook of Psychological Testing*. London: Routledge.

Chapter 1

To see '*g*' or not to see '*g*' . . .

How many types of intelligence are there?

The first question I want to address is simple. Should we talk about human intelligence – human mental abilities – as one thing or as many things: intelligence or intelligences? This question of how to conceive of human mental capacities is a vexed one. Psychologists argued about it for most of the 20th century, and the debate continues. From the non-specialist's viewpoint, they appear to do little more than coat opinion with statistical opacity. The nub of the issue is that discussions about human mental ability are a commonplace. Yet in the frequent appellations of people's being 'clever', 'smart', 'intelligent', 'bright', and 'sharp', there often exists a tension. On the one hand, we are sometimes referring to people as being generally mentally able or less so: 'What a bright guy!' Contrariwise, we sometimes pick out a special mental ability that a person has in some abundance, that appears to contrast with their otherwise modest arrangements: 'He's good with figures, but he can never remember where he puts things and he has no common sense.'

It's probably better to get in at the start a proclamation of incompleteness. In psychology we tend to measure that which can be measured. Therefore, when we discuss the mental abilities and their relations, it must be kept in mind that, if there are some qualities that we value but we feel cannot easily be measured, then our account of intelligence will be limited. For example, we are relatively poor at measuring things like creativity and wisdom, some of the most valued human attributes. What I want to do now is give an indication of the sorts of things measured in some well-known intelligence tests and ask whether these different skills are related to each other or whether they are largely distinct.

Key dataset 1

The first research story here concerns the decision by a large international psychological company to update its most comprehensive intelligence test. The job involved recruiting and testing over 2000 people in 28 American cities. Each person was tested on 13 mental tests over a total time of an hour or two. Using this dataset, the question I want to address here is: do people tend to be good at some tests and poor at others, or are people just generally good or bad at mental tests?

Before proceeding, let's be clear about the sorts of mental tasks that people were asked to do in these intelligence tests. Look at Figure 1. The first thing to notice is the 13 rectangular boxes around the bottom of the diagram. Each of these boxes has the name of a different mental test. Together the 13 tests make up a collection of tests called the Wechsler Adult Intelligence Scale, version III. This is usually just shortened to the WAIS-III. It costs many hundreds of pounds to buy and may only be bought by people with the proper credentials, for example, educational, clinical, and occupational psychologists. It can only be administered by a trained psychological tester, working one-to-one with the person being tested for up to a couple of hours. The 13 individual tests involve a wide range of mental effort for the person being tested. It is useful to describe the individual tests and some of the items so that we are not discussing this topic too abstractly. Because the tests are copyright, I describe items *like* those that appear in the test but not the actual items themselves.

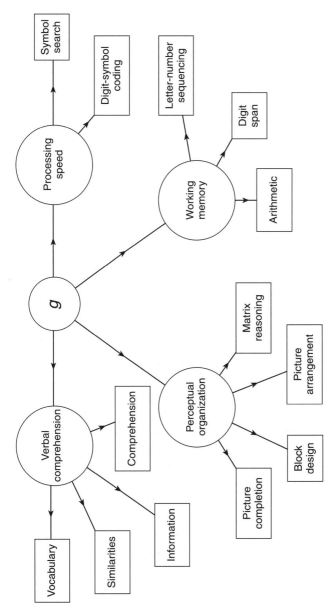

1. The hierarchy of mental ability test scores from the Wechsler Adult Intelligence Scale III.

If you were to sit the WAIS-III test, the types of mental task you would be asked to do are as follows:

Vocabulary. Tell the examiner what certain words mean. For example: chair (easy), hesitant (medium), presumptuous (hard). (33 words)

Similarities. Say what two words have in common. For example: In what way are an apple and a pear alike? In what way are a painting and a symphony alike? (19 questions)

Information. General knowledge questions covering people, places, and events. For example: How many days are in a week? What is the capital of France? Name three oceans. Who wrote *Inferno*? (28 questions)

Comprehension. Questions about everyday-life problems, aspects of society, and proverbs. For example: Tell me some reasons why we put food in a refrigerator. Why do people require driving licences? What does it mean to say 'a bird in the hand is worth two in the bush'? (18 questions)

Picture completion. Spot the missing element in a series of colour drawings. For example: that spokes are missing from one wheel in a picture of a bicycle; that one buttonhole is missing from a jacket in a picture of a person. As in the earlier tests in the collection, the questions become progressively more difficult. (25 drawings)

Block design. After looking at two-dimensional patterns made up of red and white squares and triangles, you have to reproduce these patterns using cubes with red and white faces. (14 patterns)

Picture arrangement. Given a series of cartoon drawings you must put them in an order that tells a logical story. (14 of these series)

Matrix reasoning. Find the missing element in a pattern that is built up in a logical manner. An example of this type of task is shown in Figure 2. (26 questions)

Arithmetic. Mental arithmetic problems. (20 questions)

Digit span. Repeating a sequence of numbers to the examiner. Sequences run from 2 to 9 numbers in length. An easy example is to repeat 3-7-4; harder is 3-9-1-7-4-5-3-9. In the second part of this

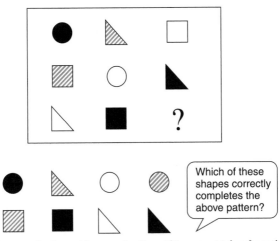

2. An example of a matrix reasoning item. This was not taken from the Wechsler Adult Intelligence Scale-III because their test materials are protected by copyright. It is an item developed for but not used in the revision to the famous Raven's Progressive Matrices test. I thank John Raven (son of the inventor of the original test) for allowing me to use this item.

types

test the sequences must be repeated in reverse order (maximum of 16 forward and 14 reversed sequences).

Letter–number sequencing. The examiner reads a series of alternate letters and numbers. You must repeat them, putting the numbers first and in numerical order, followed by the letters in alphabetical order. For example, you would repeat 'W-4-G-8-L-3' as '3–4–8–G-L-W' (maximum of 21 trials).

Digit-symbol coding. You write down the number that corresponds to a given symbol. An example of this type of task is shown in Figure 3 (as many as you can in 90 seconds).

Symbol search. You identify from a list of abstract symbols which symbol in a given pair is contained in the list (as many as you can in 2 minutes).

Some of these tests involve knowledge picked up from education, and

Key

1	2	3	4	5	6	7	8	9
>	—	≠	□	×	|	⌐	人	▽

Practice

4	8	9	1	2	6	3	5	7

Test

3	2	5	6	9	1	2	7	7

4	6	7	2	1	9	8	8	3

2	3	8	5	6	4	8	3	7

3. Part of a test that is quite like the digit-symbol coding test of the Wechsler Adult Intelligence Scale-III. The idea is to enter the code that corresponds to each number in the empty space provided. The score is the number completed in 90 seconds. In the real test there would be far more items available for completion.

some don't. Some involve language, some numbers, some shapes, and some are more abstract. Some are done at speed, within time limits, and some not. Some involve memory and some don't. Some involve reasoning with information given by the tester; some involve discovering rules; some involve articulating abstract principles; some involve practical knowledge. The tests are tapping quite a wide range of our mental functions: seeing similarities and differences, drawing inferences, working out and applying rules, remembering and manipulating mental material, working out how to construct shapes, processing information at speed, articulating the meaning of words, recalling general knowledge, explaining practical actions in everyday life, working with numbers, attending to details, and so forth. They are reasonably representative of the spread of contents scoured by IQ-type tests. Arguably, certain sorts of mental functions do seem to be poorly represented here, or not represented at all, but it is true to insist that a reasonably wide range of thinking skills gets a look-in. And, for those who wish to write these tests off as mere 'paper-and-pencil' tests, only 3 of the 13 tests require the examinee to write anything down, and none requires writing words.

The WAIS-III is developed and marketed by the Psychological Corporation in the USA and the UK. This large company develops and markets a wide range of psychological tests around the world. When they were gathering information about the WAIS-III in the USA, they tested 2450 people. These people were a fair sample of ordinary American citizens: there were equal numbers of men and women, there was a representative sample from age 16 to age 89, the ethnic and regional mix was like that of America as a whole, and there was a good spread of educational level among the people tested. Every person sat the 13 tests described above. The results of this big testing exercise saw a repeat of one of psychology's most surprising and most reproduced findings.

Before relating that finding, consider the following question. What do you expect to see in the relations (correlations) between the different tests? Perhaps some will be unrelated to each other because they tap different mental skills? A sensible guess, one that I shared before seeing data such as these, is that many of these mental functions have no relations with each other. That is, there might be no relationship between performance on some individual tests and on others. One might go further and guess that being good at some tasks might carry a price in being poor at others – this predicts a negative correlation between some tests. For example, people with better ability to see spatial patterns might have lower verbal ability. Or those who can see small, pernickety details in pictures might be poorer when to comes to checking through lists at speed. Or perhaps people with good memories have a slower mental speed. A lot of our intuitive thinking about mental capability runs along the lines of there being some cost for any mental benefit we possess.

In fact, none of those predictions is correct. The fact is that every single one of those 13 tests in the WAIS-III has a positive correlation with every other one. People who are better at any one test *tend* to be better at all of the others. There are 78 correlations when we look at all the pairings among the 13 tests. Every single correlation is positive – a good score on one of the tests tends to bring with it a good score on the others. There are no tests unrelated to any other one, i.e. there are no near-to-zero correlations. There are no tests that are negatively related with other ones. Even the *lowest* correlation between any two tests is still a modest 0.3 (between picture completion and digit span). The highest – between vocabulary and information – is almost 0.8. The average correlation is 0.5. Thus, even the average correlation between these rather different mental tests is on the large side.

The first substantial fact, then, is that all of these different tests show positive associations – people good at one tend to be good at all of the others. But remember that we are talking about the tendencies within this large group of people; individuals provide us with comforting exceptions.

The second important fact is that some sub-groups of tests in the WAIS-III collection associate higher among themselves than with others. For example, the tests of vocabulary, information, similarities, and comprehension all have especially high associations with each other. So, although they relate quite strongly to *every* test in the WAIS-III collection, they form a little pool of tests that are especially highly related among themselves. The same thing occurs with digit span, arithmetic, and letter–number sequencing. They relate positively with all of the other tests in the collection, but they relate especially highly with each other.

This is not so surprising. The four former tests all involve language, learning, and understanding. The three latter tests involve numbers and the ability to hold facts in memory while manipulating them. Within the

WAIS-III collection of tests there are four such pools of tests that have especially close associations among themselves, even though they still relate positively to all the others. These pools of tests are indicated in Figure 1. Note that a circle with the label 'verbal comprehension' has arrows pointing to four tests: Vocabulary, information, similarities, and comprehension. What this means is that there are such close associations among these tests that they can be collected together under a hypothetical entity called 'verbal comprehension'. This entity merely captures the fact that these four tests have closer associations among themselves than they do with other tests. There is no test called 'verbal comprehension' – it is a statistical distillation of these four individual tests. It recognizes their especially close correlations.

There are three other collections of tests within the WAIS-III that seem to hang together especially tightly. In Figure 1 the closely associated picture completion, block design, picture arrangement, and matrix reasoning tests are collected under the heading 'perceptual organization', a label that seems quite nicely to capture the sorts of thinking we must do to perform well on these tests.

The three tests that involve numbers are collected under the heading 'working memory'. Working memory is a label that psychologists use to describe the ability to hold information in memory and manipulate it at the same time. Imagine someone asking you a series of quite complicated questions to which you must give an answer. Imagine, in addition, that you were concurrently being asked to remember the last word in each question as well, so that you could write down the list later. Thus, at the same time as trying to answer each question in turn you'd be trying to remember a list of isolated words. That would hurt your head and the facility under strain would be what psychologists call your 'working memory'.

Finally, there are two tests that have a high association and both involve working at speed to make comparisons with visual symbols. They have been collected under the label 'processing speed'.

To recap. A collection of 13 varied mental tests given to over 2000 adult Americans has shown that the ability to perform well on all of these tests is related. In addition, there are sub-groups of tests that relate more highly to each other than to the other tests. In Figure 1 we illustrate this latter fact by showing the related groups of tests collected together under headings or labels that summarize the sorts of mental skills common to the tests. In fact, the common name for these four collections of sub-groups is 'group factors'. These group factors refer to certain domains of cognitive performance that can be separated to a degree. The statistical methods used to examine these data can give people scores on 'verbal comprehension', 'perceptual organization', 'working memory', and 'processing speed'.

Just as was done on the 13 individual test scores, we can go further and measure the correlations among these four group factors. That is, we can ask whether someone who is good at one of these group factors of mental ability tends to be good at all the others. For example, do people with good 'working memory' scores also have fast 'processing speed', good 'verbal comprehension' scores, and good 'perceptual organization' scores? The answer is an even more emphatic yes: these four group factors have correlations between 0.60 and 0.80. These are large associations and they mark the fact that people who tend to be skilled in one of these group factors tend to be skilled in all of the others. People tend generally to be good or poor at all of the tests and all of the group factors. This is shown in Figure 1 by having all of the group factors collected under a single heading of '*g*', which, under an old convention, stands for the general factor in human intelligence. Once again, it is a statistical distillation that describes a solid research finding: that there is something shared by all the tests in terms of people's tendencies to do well, modestly, or poorly on all of them.

What comes next is very important. The rectangles in Figure 1 are actual mental tests – the 13 sub-tests – that make up the Wechsler collection. The four circles that represent the 'group factors' and the circle that contains g are optimal ways of representing the statistical associations among the tests contained in the rectangles. The things in the circles, the specific/group factor abilities and 'g', do not equate to things in the human mind – they are not bits of the brain. The names we pencil into the circles are our common-sense guesses about what seems to be common to the sub-groups of tests that associate closely. The circles themselves emerged from the statistical procedures and the data, not from intuition about the tests' similarities, but the labels we give the circles have to be decided by common sense. Again, the names of factors in the circles in Figure 1 are our ways of conceptualizing types of performance on mental tests. That is not to say that we will never discover what the brain systems are which do these sorts of mental tasks, but we cannot claim such a thing based on these data. You will sometimes catch me referring to people's 'verbal ability' or their 'working memory' or whatever. What I am referring to is people's performance on this or that type of mental test. I am not trying to sell you a model of the human brain. Of course, it is interesting to ask how the brain manages to execute different types of mental work, and we cover some of that research in Chapter 3. But it is important to appreciate that the analysis of mental tests that we deal with here just classifies the tests' statistical associations: it does not discover the systems into which the brain partitions its activities.

This way of describing human mental capabilities, as illustrated in Figure 1, is called a hierarchy. It illustrates the fact that mental abilities as measured in mental tests tend to collect together in pools that have especially close associations. It also notes the fact that these pools themselves are all highly related. When we think about individual differences in people's abilities, therefore, the message from this large study is that about half of the variability in a large group of adults may be attributed to mental ability that is required to perform all tests – g or 'general intelligence'. Thus it does make sense to refer to a general type of mental ability; talking about a single, general intelligence has some veracity. There is something common to people's performance differences across many types of mental test. Next, we can say with confidence that there is more to human mental ability than just being *generally* clever. We see from Figure 1 that there are special types of ability and that these can be described in terms of the kinds of specific mental work needed to perform certain tests. Last, the combination of general ability and group factors is not enough to account for how well people perform on the 13 tests of the WAIS-III. There seems to be very specific ability needed to do well on each test, something that is not shared with any other test even where the material in the test is quite similar to that in other tests.

In thinking about how efficient your own mental machinery is you would need to consider at least 3 questions. First, how strong is my general ability? Second, what are my strengths and weaknesses on the group factors? Third, are there some very specific tests on which I excel? I hope that brings some order to the question of how many human abilities there are. The answer is that it depends on what level of specificity you have in mind.

The first person to describe the general factor in human intelligence was an English army officer turned psychologist, Charles Spearman, in a famous research paper in 1904. He examined schoolchildren's scores on different academic subjects. The scores were all positively correlated and he put this down to a general mental ability. There followed decades of arguments among psychologists as to whether or not there was such a single entity. American psychologists, notably Louis Thurstone, suggested that there were about 7 separate human abilities. Although the argument raged on, and still does to an extent, it became clear by the 1940s that, whenever a group of people was tested on a collection of mental tests, the correlations among the test scores were almost entirely positive and the general factor in mental ability was a significant, inescapable fact. Just how significant is the *g* factor was described above: it accounts for about half of the variability in mental ability in the general population. Just how inescapable it is became clear in the early 1990s.

Key dataset 2

In 1993 the American psychologist John Carroll brought out his book *Human Cognitive Abilities: A Survey of Factor Analytic Studies*. His long career in academic psychology saw him through most of the debates about the number and nature of human mental abilities. He saw that there was disagreement and that there were some barriers to coming to a consensus. One problem was that there were hundreds of studies that had tested people on mental ability tests. They tended to use different numbers and types of test. The people tested in the studies were of different ages and backgrounds. The researchers used different statistical methods to help them decide on their conclusions. Carroll's purpose was to retrieve as many of the studies on human intelligence conducted during the 20th century as he considered to be of good quality. He then re-analysed all of these studies using the same statistical methods. This involved re-analysing over 400 sets of data, which included most of the large, well-known collections of data on human mental ability testing from the period. Therefore, if one knows what Carroll reported, one knows most of the well-known data ever collected on human intelligence differences.

Carroll's results were reported in his 800+-page book, brim-full of statistical analyses and technical jargon. The essence of his findings appears on his page 626, a diagram he called his 'three stratum model' of human cognitive ability. A simpler version of it is reproduced as Figure 4 here. It has a structure very similar to the one in Figure 1. At the top of his hierarchy is his 'stratum III', or 'general intelligence' as he termed it. At 'stratum II' there are 8 broad types of mental ability, 4 of which are similar to those group factors/specific abilities we found

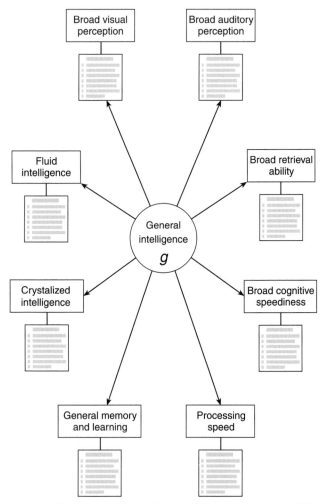

4. A hierarchical representation of the associations among mental ability test scores. This diagram was the result of decades of work by John B. Carroll who re-analysed over 400 large, classic databases on human intelligence research.

earlier, in the WAIS-III. Carroll found more because he looked at data sets that included more, and more different, types of ability than those in the WAIS-III collection. At 'stratum I' – shown here as lists of grey lines – there were very specific mental skills, much like the ones specific to individual ability tests such as those we saw in the WAIS-III. Again, as we found with the WAIS-III data, Carroll's strata of mental abilities emerged as an optimal result from a standardized statistical procedure, not from his imposing a structure on the data. He *discovered* rather than *invented* the hierarchy of intelligence differences.

What research is currently going on in this area?

Among psychologists working in this field there is no longer any substantial debate about the structure of human mental ability differences. Something like John Carroll's three-stratum model almost always appears from a collection of mental tests. A general factor emerges that accounts for about half of the individual differences among the scores for a group of people, and there are group factors that are narrower abilities, and then very specific factors below that. Therefore, we can nowadays describe the structure of mental test performances quite reliably, but this is not proven to represent a model of the organization and compartments of the human brain.

The principal dissidents from this well-supported view are on the semi-popular fringes of scientific psychology. Howard Gardner's popular writings on 'multiple intelligences' have suggested that there are many forms of mental ability and that they are unrelated. The facts are that some of Gardner's supposedly separate intelligences are well known to be correlated positively and linked thereby to general mental ability, such as his verbal, mathematical, and musical intelligences. Some of his so-called intelligences, though valued human attributes, are not normally considered to be mental abilities, i.e. not within man's 'cognitive' sphere. For example, physical intelligence is a set of motor skills and interpersonal intelligence involves personality traits.

What no one doubts is that tests of mental abilities do not assess all important aspects of brain function, let alone all important human qualities. They do not measure creativity or wisdom. Neither of these is easy to measure, though both have some demonstrable associations with intelligence. Mental ability tests do not measure personality, social adroitness, leadership, charisma, cool-headedness, altruism, or many other things that we value. But that proper point is not the same as saying that they are useless.

To follow this area up. . .

The information for this chapter was taken mostly from the two following research-level sources, which mostly address intelligence from the viewpoint of mental ability tests:

Carroll, J. B. (1993). *Human Cognitive Abilities: A Survey of Factor Analytic Studies*. Cambridge, UK: Cambridge University Press.
Wechsler, D. (1997). *Manual for the Wechsler Adult Intelligence Scale-III*. New York: Psychological Corporation.

For something more engaging that deals with a wider range of human mental capabilities, I recommend the well written (if contentious):

Gardner, H. (1983, reissued 1993). *Frames of Mind: The Theory of Multiple Intelligences*. New York: Basic Books.

If you enjoy this and want an update on how Gardner has elaborated his ideas since the 1980s, then have a look at his follow-up.

Gardner, H. (1999). *Intelligence Reframed: Multiple Intelligences for the 21st Century*. New York: Basic Books.

Two documents recording agreement among researchers in the field about the core aspects of human intelligence (and see the last chapter for further agreement in a third important document) are also worth looking at. The first was, rather astonishingly, a full-page declaration in the *Wall Street Journal* on 13 December 1994. It was a list of 25 statements summarizing what is known about human intelligence, signed by 52 well-known researchers (including John Carroll). Its first statement was:

> Intelligence is a very general mental capability that, among other things, involves the ability to reason, plan, solve problems, think abstractly, comprehend complex ideas, learn quickly and learn from experience. It is not merely book learning, a narrow academic skill, or test-taking smarts. Rather, it reflects a broader and deeper capability for comprehending our surroundings – 'catching on', 'making sense' of things, or 'figuring out' what to do.

The statement was expanded upon, with details of its history and a useful bibliography, as an editorial in the journal *Intelligence*:

Gottfredson, L. S. (1997). Mainstream science on intelligence: an editorial with 52 signatories, history, and bibliography. *Intelligence*, 24, 13–23.

Another source of guidance for those who want some verbal formulation of human intelligence is the following book.

Snyderman, M. & S. Rothman (1988). *The IQ Controversy, the Media and Public Policy*. New Brunswick: Transaction Books.

Snyderman and Rothman polled experts concerning their views on human intelligence and its measurement. The majority of the experts agreed – a substantial minority disagreed – that there was a consensus among psychologists and educators as to the kinds of behaviours that are labelled 'intelligent'. What emerged, though, was near unanimity about the core aspects of intelligence, and a tapering-off in agreement on some facets of human performance that I already noted to be problematic. Here are the aspects of human behaviour they were asked to rate, with the percentage of experts who thought each aspect was an important element of intelligence.

Abstract thinking or reasoning	99.3%
Problem-solving ability	97.7%
Capacity to acquire knowledge	96.0%

Compared with this near-unanimous agreement on aspects of intelligence, 'memory' was endorsed as an important element of intelligence by 80.5%, mental speed by 71.7%, general knowledge by 62.4%, creativity by 59.6%, and achievement motivation by only 18.9%.

Chapter 2

Ageing and intelligence: senility or sagacity?

What happens to mental abilities as we grow older?

Most people of middle and old age are willing to concede that their physical prowess in many areas was not what it was when they were in their 20s and 30s. Similarly, they sometimes complain with a hint of humour that their memory is not what it was. It's an interesting fact of life, though, that one hardly ever hears people complain about their worsening intelligence as they grow older.

Asking about the ageing of human intelligence means asking at least two different questions. First, how stable are the individual differences among people as they move from childhood through adulthood to old age? The interest here is in whether those at the top and the bottom stay there or whether there is more change, with people who used to perform poorly in early life doing better later on, and vice versa. That is, is the rank order of people's mental ability in our school classroom still the same when that class meets again at retirement or even later?

Second, is there on average a tendency for people to lose mental power as they grow old? This is a question about what old age does to people on the whole. That is, on average, do the people in our school classroom decline to a degree below their peak mental function in their young adulthood?

These questions are now addressed in turn.

Key dataset 3

Have a look at Figure 5. It's called a 'scattergram', a diagram with a scatter of points. Each point on the diagram represents a person. In fact each is a combination of two numbers relating to that person. The horizontal shows the score that a given person obtained the first time they took a certain mental test. The vertical shows the score that the person obtained the second time they took the test. The diagonal line in the diagram is the line along which all the points would rest if mental test scores were perfectly stable over time – that is, if every person got the same score the first and second time they tried the test all the points would fall on that line.

They don't. The points deviate from that pattern of perfect stability in two ways. First, notice that most of the points fall above the diagonal

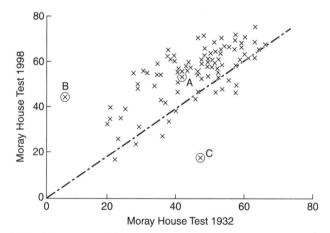

5. A scattergram graph that compares people's scores on the Moray House Test in 1932 (at age 11) and in 1998 (at age 77). Some crosses represent more than one person.

line. That means that most people scored better the second time they took the test: the group, on average, improved over time. (That could just mean that they had more practice on the second occasion, and that they recalled some of the questions and were generally better prepared and less anxious about the test. When more details about these data are revealed it will become clear that this is unlikely.) Second, note that there is a general pattern of points flowing from the bottom left of the graph to the top right. There aren't many points in the top left or bottom right of the graph's area. But notice, too, that there is some spread, so that the correlation is not perfect. Some people did better than their first score and some did a bit worse, but there is still quite a strong tendency for the people who did well first time round to do better on the second test. We'll discuss a bit more about what these data mean after describing the way in which the researchers did the testing.

On the morning of 1 June 1932 everyone in Scotland who was born in 1921 and who was at school sat a mental ability test. In a massive national exercise that has never been repeated in any other country in the world, the entire population of $10\frac{1}{2}$- to $11\frac{1}{2}$-year-olds took the same intelligence test under the same conditions. It was organized by the Scottish Council for Research in Education and it was called the Scottish Mental Survey 1932. The survey data were to assist in educational provision and to measure the amounts of mental handicap in schools. Teachers did the testing and the scoring of the tests. The test was provided by the then-famous educational psychologist Sir Godfrey Thomson from the University of Edinburgh, the originator of the Moray House Tests which were used in the UK as '11-plus' tests for selection into different types of secondary school. The test used in the Scottish Mental Survey 1932 was a variation on one of the Moray House Tests. So, for 45 minutes on a summer's morning in 1932, exactly 87,498 children applied their brainpower to questions about words, sentences, numbers, shapes, codes, instructions, and other miscellaneous mental tasks.

Until about the 1960s the Scottish Mental Surveys (another one was done in 1947, on the people born in 1936) were famous for their completeness, and several scholarly books were published with the statistical data from them. However, as the 11-year-olds from 1932 reached middle and old age, the data gathered dust in a series of Edinburgh attics and basements. Psychologists interested in the study of human intelligence differences had all but forgotten about the results of the Scottish Mental Surveys.

In the summer of 1996, Lawrence Whalley (from the Department of Mental Health, University of Aberdeen) called me (at the Department of Psychology, University of Edinburgh) to ask whether there might be some mileage in administering some mental tests to the Aberdeen Birth Cohort 1921. This group of people was being studied for signs of cardiovascular disease, and Professor Whalley wanted to know whether heart disease reduced intelligence levels. Not really, was my reply, because, without prior mental test data on these people that was collected before their illness started, information on current mental ability would not tell us about relative changes in cognition as a result of disease. However, coincidentally, at that time I was reading Richard Lynn's book *Dysgenics* (1996, published by Praeger), which referred to a study conducted by the Scottish Council for Research in Education (SCRE) on people born in 1921. I called Lawrence Whalley back: the Aberdeen cohort might indeed be worth retesting, because many of them probably did have their mental ability tested at age 11 years in the Scottish Mental Survey 1932. This was the sequence of accidents that led to his tracking down the Survey data to a safe bunker in SCRE's offices in St John's Street, Edinburgh. In a series of heavy ledgers and brown paper packages tied up with string, the more than 60-year-old data were preserved, recorded in the neat copperplate script of the 1930s teachers. Each region of Scotland had its own ledgers. Each of the region's schools had its own pages in the ledger. And each line of each ledger contained a pupil's name, date of birth, and mental ability test score.

As we literally blew dust from these ledgers, it began to sink in just how valuable were these data. In recent years the Western world's populations have changed, with a higher proportion of older people. It has emerged that one of the determinants of high quality of life in old age is avoiding cognitive decline. But to find out whether people have or have not retained their intellectual abilities one needs to know what people used to be like. Though there are some studies that have followed up people as they grow older, none has been able to relate ability in childhood to ability in old age. Before the re-emergence of the data from the Scottish Mental Survey 1932, there were almost no data looking at change in mental ability over the whole human lifespan.

Our first aim was now to discover how stable intelligence was from age 11 to age 77. We set about trying to find some of the still-healthy people who took part in the Scottish Mental Survey 1932. Advertisements were placed in the media and our researchers contacted people via their general medical practitioners. We hired Aberdeen's Music Hall for the morning of 1 June 1998 and set it out as an examination hall. Crucially, we obtained a copy of the original Moray House Test that was used in 1932 and had it reprinted. Only a couple of tiny changes to two questions were needed to prevent anachronisms in the test. Exactly 66 years to the day after they first sat the test, 73 people came along to re-sit the test that they had last seen as young schoolchildren (Figures 6 and 7). A meeting some weeks later increased our numbers to 101. The instructions were read out exactly as they had been in 1932 and the same time limit was applied.

The results we found are summarized in Figure 5. Most people scored better at age 77 than they had done in 1932 at age 11, but that is not the main point. The important finding is that, largely speaking, the people who did well in 1932 also tended to do well in 1998. Those who did more poorly as children tended to stay near the bottom. Most people fall along a line which indicates general consistency in scores. The

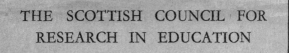

THE SCOTTISH COUNCIL FOR
RESEARCH IN EDUCATION

1932

MENTAL SURVEY
TEST

SUITABLE FOR PUPILS OF
TEN AND ELEVEN YEARS OF AGE

MENTAL SURVEY TEST, 8 pp., 4d.
PRELIMINARY PRACTICE TEST, 2 pp., 1d.
INSTRUCTIONS FOR ADMINISTRATION,
8 pp., 4d.

SPECIMEN SET - *9d., post free*

UNIVERSITY OF LONDON PRESS Ltd.
WAR-TIME ADDRESS:
ST HUGH'S SCHOOL, BICKLEY, KENT

6. Cover of the Moray House Test used in the Scottish Mental Survey 1932.

7. Photograph of members of the Scottish Mental Survey 1932 returning after 66 years to sit the same mental test they had taken at age 11. The venue is the Music Hall in Aberdeen, the date 1 June 1998.

correlation was greater than 0.6, which is large. As an added technicality, the people we got back to take the test in 1998 were not fully representative of the whole population. On average they were better test scorers than the full population and they tended not to have such a wide spread in scores. This narrowing of the range of scores lowers our correlation from the true value, and it seems that 0.7 might be nearer to the mark than 0.6 over 66 years.

Note the points marked A, B, and C in Figure 5. Person A has about an average score at age 11 and again at age 77. B and C are the two people who show the most dramatic inconsistencies between 1932 and 1998. Person B has an average score in 1998, but a very poor score when tested in school 66 years earlier. Person C had an average score in 1932 but was equal-lowest when we tested people in 1998, representing a dramatic drop in relative performance.

What these results mean is that there is a large amount of stability overall, and about an equal amount of change, in our relative levels of mental ability from early adolescence to old age. Looking again at Figure 5 we see that the points are far from describing an exact straight line. That means that there is a considerable amount of change. Some people improve and some decline with age; many change their rank order in the group. The sources of these continuities and changes in this important area of our mental lives are being sought by many current researchers. Sadly, for example, we discovered later that Person C in Figure 5 was in the early stages of Alzheimer's dementia.

In summary, the answer to the first question about age and intelligence is that there is a substantial stability in the rank-ordering of human intelligence across the human lifespan, and also substantial change. There is substantial change because the correlation coefficient measuring stability is far from perfect.

Key dataset 4

The psychologist K. Werner Schaie wanted to find out whether people's mental abilities changed with age: not so much whether individual people stayed at the same level in a rank order, but whether the average level of ability improved or declined with age. He used a complicated procedure of testing in order to find out. It requires some digression to explain why less elaborate studies were inadequate. Obviously, the Scottish data I described above are unsuitable: at age 11 years intelligence has still not reached its adult peak and so, at age 77, the people from the Scottish Mental Survey 1932 did better but were not being compared with their best-ever performance.

One way to find out whether people of different ages have different levels of mental ability is to go out and test thousands of people of different ages on the same battery of mental tests. It would be important to make sure that people at each age level were representative of the whole population. It would be inappropriate just to examine brighter older people versus duller younger ones. With this proviso, the great benefit of this type of test is that it can be done quickly, at one point in time. In fact, there are many data of this type. The norms from the well-known test batteries, like the Wechsler test, for example (see Chapter 1), tell a clear story. For some of the tests in the Wechsler battery there is little change with age: older people do just as well as younger people on some tests. On those tests that measure vocabulary, general information, or verbal reasoning, there is little or no age-related decrement in ability. For those tests that are timed or time restricted, more abstract, or require reasoning about spatial relationships, there are marked decrements with age: younger people out-perform older ones. The USA's Department of Labor tested over 30,000 people in the workplace on the General Aptitude Test Battery, and found much the same – that there was little change between age 20 and 60+ on abilities like vocabulary, and that there was a straight decline from age 20 to age 60 on tests of abstract and spatial reasoning, especially when these had to be done at speed.

This type of study is called a 'cross-sectional' study, when different ages are measured at the same time. It faces major problems of interpretation. The people of different ages who are being compared do not share the same educational, nutritional, medical, or cultural histories. Any differences between the ages might well be caused by these factors rather than age per se.

So, some psychologists have taken on the challenge of doing longitudinal studies: that is, they test people when they are young and then again when they are old(er). Two of the most remarkable studies are from North America and are related to the testing that went on during military recruitment for the two world wars. W. A. Owens tested over 100 American men in 1950 and 1961 after finding their 'Army alpha' scores from 1919. The Army alpha was the first-ever group test of intelligence devised for adults, and was developed for recruitment of American men into the army in World War I. Owens found that, 30 and 40 years later, the men were just as good at verbal ability and almost as good at numerical ability, but had slipped quite a bit from their young adult scores on abstract reasoning. These are similar to the findings of the cross-sectional studies. Comparable results are found, too, in the Concordia University study which has retested a few hundred men 40 years after their original test on recruitment to the Canadian armed services in World War II. They were just as good at age 65 as they were at 25 on verbal ability, but much poorer on non-verbal ability. Reasoning under speed concerning the logical relations of abstract shapes declines especially clearly as people grow older.

However, these longitudinal studies have problems too. They might be much harder to carry out than cross-sectional studies, not least because you might have to wait several decades to conduct one. Inevitably, not everyone comes back to be tested some years later. Some people die, some become ill, some move away, some cannot be found, and others just refuse to take part. The ones that do come back are not a representative group, and the results obtained from them cannot be generalized to the whole population. Another problem is that any group of people who were born in about the same calendar year go through a sequence of human experiences – medical, cultural, educational, and so forth – that are unique to that cohort of people, again making their results not necessarily generalizable. Whatever decline is found might apply only to that group of people undergoing their particular life histories. Last and greatest, though, of the problems that beset the great effort that goes into longitudinal studies is that of practice. When people take a test for a second time they might be doing better than we should otherwise expect because they have done it before. This can mask any effects of ageing.

To counter some of the problems of cross-sectional and longitudinal studies, Schaie began a cross-sequential study in Seattle. Figure 8 illustrates the design of this study. His participants were members of a medical insurance scheme. The Figure's left-hand side has the dates when people were tested, in 1956 and every 7 years thereafter until 1991. There are 6 grey columns in the Figure, each shorter than the last. In the first of these columns in the Figure, the number 500 at the bottom shows that in 1956 Schaie recruited 500 people. These people ranged in age from the late teens to 80s. They were tested on various mental tests to cover key mental abilities at the stratum II level (see Figure 4). This is a standard cross-sectional study: a number of people with different ages are tested on some intelligence tests at one point in time and they are compared to see whether older people differ from younger people in the scores they obtain.

Progressing up this first column in Figure 8, we see that Schaie called back these people every 7 years to retake the same tests. Thus, he used

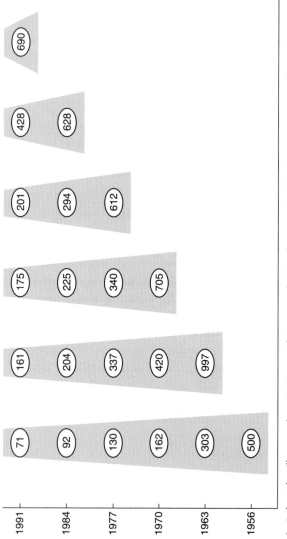

8. A chart that illustrates how K. Werner Schaie set up the Seattle Longitudinal Study to examine the effects of age on intelligence.

his original cross-sectional study of 500 people to conduct a longitudinal study. Note that, as time moves through the 1960s to the early 1990s the numbers fall from several hundred in 1963 to only 71 in 1991. As noted above, some people die, some get ill, some move away, and some just can't, or don't want to, come back.

Schaie added an interesting twist, making the study much more useful and, especially as time went on, more burdensome to organize. Look at the second grey column of Figure 8. In 1963, when the people from the 1956 sample were coming back to be tested for a second time, Schaie recruited a new group of participants, to be tested for the first time. The second grey column of Figure 8 shows that he collected data on 997 completely new subjects. These people, again, were aged from their late teens to their 80s, and were given the same tests every 7 years from then on. Schaie's approach is now obvious. He collected a completely *new* group of several hundred people (aged from late teens to 80-something) every 7 years and asked back and tested all the old groups as well. Every 7 years, then, each of the groups already recruited was asked back to be tested again, and a new sample was collected.

All this means three things. *One*: the bottom of every one of the grey columns in Figure 8 marks a new cross-sectional study of ageing and intelligence. This informs us about the age-related differences in mental abilities in samples taken from different decades of the second half of the 20th century. *Two*: each column of Figure 8 is a new longitudinal study, which allows some judgement to be made about whether the results from any one longitudinal study are able to be repeated. *Three*: most crucially, this type of study allows one thing that neither a cross-sectional or a longitudinal study alone can do. *We can compare people of the same ages at different years in history*. Thus, Schaie's design allows us to ask the question of whether, say, 20-year-olds (or 30-, 40-, or 50-, and so forth) in 1956 score the same as 20-year-olds (or whatever) in 1963, 1970, 1977, 1984, and so on. This key question is called a 'cohort' effect, and is looked at in more detail in Key dataset 10 (Chapter 6).

As you will appreciate, it is not easy to summarize the Seattle study, because of the large amount of data it produced and the fact that it has been reporting results for over 30 years. However, some aspects may be summarized briefly. The 'cohort' effects do exist, with later generations scoring better than their predecessors at the same age (see Key dataset 10 in Chapter 6). The longitudinal aspects of the study do show practice effects on the tests. The cross-sectional data show a fairly straight decline from age 25 to 80 years in inductive reasoning (discovering a rule from a limited number of instances), spatial orientation (making decisions about complex shapes in two or three dimensions), perceptual speed (the ability to notice fine visual details quickly), and verbal memory. There was a peak in middle age, and much less age-related decline in verbal and numerical ability. Figure 9 shows some

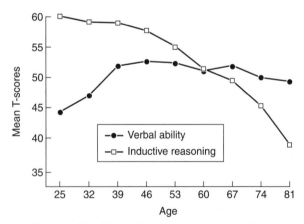

9. Not all aspects of intelligence show the same patterns of ageing. Examples of two test results from K. Werner Schaie's Seattle Longitudinal Study. Inductive reasoning – working out general rules from specific examples – declines with age from some point in the 30s. Verbal ability shows no appreciable decline with age.

quite typical results from Schaie's study. Verbal ability peaks in the 30s and stays stable until old age. Inductive, abstract reasoning declines from young adulthood to old age.

It is possible to put together all of the studies we have discussed so far concerning the ageing of intelligence and make some general conclusions. There are common characteristics of those tests that are stable over age and those that show decrements. Tests on which we can all hope to be performing well in our old age are those that involve knowledge or educational experience and draw generally from our stores of knowledge. These are called 'crystallized' abilities by psychologists, and the metaphor is used to indicate that we have formed the knowledge solidly in our brains. A good example of such a test is vocabulary.

Tests on which people beyond their 30s are typically already past their peak are those that involve more on-the-spot thinking, with novel material, and often completed under pressure of time. These are called 'fluid' abilities, indicating that they represent the current state of our brainpower. The distinction between fluid and crystallized intelligence was noted by John Horn and Raymond Cattell in the 1960s. A good example of a fluid ability test is Raven's Progressive Matrices, in which one must find the correct example to finish an abstract pattern (an example was given in Figure 2). Thus, as a broad generalization, the tests which show decrements with ageing are those that involve speedy, active brainpower with ideas that we have never seen before. The tests that hold better with ageing are those that call upon our stored knowledge retrieved at our leisure. You might think of this distinction as ways of enquiring about the output of a factory. This could be done in two ways. You could go to the shop floor and ask to see the on-the-spot manufacture of some new products. This would tell you about the factory's current ability to make new objects, about the present capability and current efficiency of its machinery: *fluid intelligence*. On the other hand, you could ask to be taken to the warehouse to see the quality and quantity of the products it has accumulated over its active lifespan: *crystallized intelligence*. On this type of thinking, Paul Baltes, an eminent researcher on the ageing of human mental abilities, made the following distinction. He called our present mental capabilities the 'mechanics' of our intelligence and our stored knowledge the 'pragmatics' of our intelligence. His decades of research in Germany, with the Berlin Aging Study and others, shows that old age reduces the mechanics, but the pragmatics hold up well as we grow old.

Thus, if we try to answer the question 'does intelligence decline with age?' we must answer in both the affirmative and the negative simultaneously, depending on the type of ability that is being discussed.

Let's go back to Schaie's Seattle study and discuss some more of their data. Apart from merely asking what types of ability do and do not change as we age, he noticed and wondered why some people seemed to preserve their thinking skills better than others as they grew older. This is a well-known phenomenon, but often overlooked. We tend to discuss the young and the old as if they were just one mass of each, with no individual differences. What Schaie's study and others find is that there are large differences in mental ability changes with age: some people decline, some stay the same, and some even improve. Perhaps there is more human interest in this one question than most others: what are the factors that will help us to retain our mental abilities as we grow older? Can we buck the general ageing trend of our peers? What, then, predicts favourable cognitive ageing? Schaie found that the following factors contributed to holding on to one's mental abilities:

- having no cardiovascular or other chronic disease
- living in a favourable environment mediated by high social class
- being involved in a complex and intellectually stimulating environment
- possessing a flexible personality style in midlife

- living with a spouse with high mental ability
- maintaining a fast level of processing speed in the brain
- being satisfied with life in middle age

Key dataset 5

The question I shall address now is: what exactly is it that declines when we say that mental ability declines with age? Let's address those mental abilities that do show some decline with age: there are many of them. If we look through all of the research reports we can show that hundreds of types of individual mental test scores decline as we grow older. However, the first two Key datasets in Chapter 1 gave us a way to think about ageing and mental abilities. We can ask whether it is mostly the stratum III general factor that changes as we grow older, and/or particular stratum II group factors, like memory, spatial ability, processing speed, verbal reasoning, and/or specific abilities that live on stratum I. Therefore, psychologists are faced, potentially, with having to come up with an account of how many different abilities age, and providing a mechanism for each.

The leviathan in this field of research is Timothy Salthouse and Figure 10 captures his ideas, though the diagram is taken from one of the reports from the Berlin Study of Aging (details at the end). Let me give the punchline first and work backwards from it to the supporting data. Salthouse believes, after examining many data over more than three decades, first that age affects the general factor in mental ability and nothing much else. The fact that very specific mental abilities (stratum I in Chapter 1) or group factors (stratum II) show age-related changes, says Salthouse, is mostly because they relate to the general intelligence factor. Second, he believes, after examining much more data, that the decline of the general factor with age is mostly caused by a slowing of speed of mental processing.

Figure 10 will be our guide to this research area. Have a look at it. Note

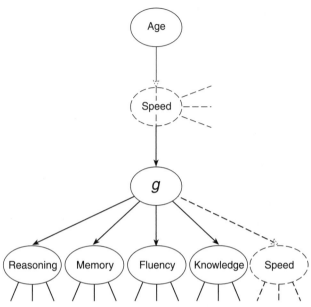

Intelligence

10. A drawing to illustrate that the effect of age on specific mental skills acts via the effect of age on general mental ability. Some researchers think that the effect of age on general mental ability is due to a slowing of the brain's processing speed.

that I have put speed in dotted lines. That's because it might be best placed in one of two different locations in the diagram. At the bottom of the Figure are several lines sticking out from 5 ellipses (familiar from Figures 1 and 4). They are types of mental ability (stratum II or group factors) and the lines sticking out are some different, individual tests that can be used to test them. I have given the stratum II mental abilities these specific names because they occurred in one particular research paper; however, the results are similar across most studies even when they examined other mental domains. Note that reasoning, memory, fluency, knowledge, and speed all have lines pointing to them from *g* (stratum III or general ability). This illustrates what we saw earlier, that almost all types of ability have positive relations with each other: people who are good at one tend to be good at all the others. Salthouse then asked an interesting question.

When we look at all those mental abilities that change with age, what does age affect? That is, does age affect general ability or does it have discrete effects on individual abilities? Perhaps, for example, it affects memory more than fluency, or reasoning more than knowledge, or perhaps speed in particular? These questions can be tested, but the statistical armoury that tests them is beyond my wit to explain here. However, the idea of the thing can be got across. Have a look at Figure 10 again. What Salthouse did was to assume that age affected *only* the general mental ability *g*. He was then able to ask whether that accounted for *all* the effects of age on the more specific mental ability test scores, or whether there were still substantial age effects that leaked over to the group factors and individual tests. The answer was clear: the effects of age were almost entirely and *only* on general ability. Once that was taken into account, there was almost no effect of age on the more narrow mental capabilities.

This very simple idea worked for many datasets that Salthouse analysed, including banks of other people's data. And others, such as researchers in the large Berlin Study of Aging, found the same results (it is one of their diagrams that I used as a model for this Figure). So, what the Figure tells us is that age alters *g* (general ability) and that it is this change in general ability that affects all the different mental abilities we recognize. The reason that 'reasoning', 'memory', 'fluency', and 'knowledge' changed with age was because they were related to general ability; it was general ability that aged, not something special about any one of these group/special ability factors. Note that I refer to 'change' rather than decline. Although it is the case that on average these abilities will go down with age, some people within the groups stay the same or even get a bit better.

What does this result mean? It means that what ages when we talk of intelligence ageing is something very general – some broad capability of the brain to handle ideas is changing, not just specific aspects of mental function. Salthouse then asked why this should be. It is not enough to say that growing older causes mental changes, especially in general mental ability. We have to try to be more specific: we must think about what physically changes in the brain as we grow older to produce these effects. His guess was that all these abilities seem to change together because our 'mental speed' is slowing down as we get older. Therefore, his bold theory is that: (1) age causes slowing of mental speed (sometimes called speed of the processing of information); (2) this change in mental speed is the cause of the change in general ability; and (3) the change in general mental ability causes the change in many different, more specific abilities, like memory and so forth.

We need to have a word about how he and others in this field have measured mental speed. Sometimes they use mental tests that are part of intelligence test batteries. For example, a test called 'digit symbol' is sometimes used as a putative index of mental speed. It belongs in the Wechsler test collection we saw in Chapter 1 and is illustrated in Figure 3. The person has to write a symbol below a number according to a given code. Therefore, for each item in the test, the person looks at the number, looks over to the code, notices the little symbol that corresponds with the given number, and writes that symbol below the number. They do as many as they can in a given time. Older people tend to get fewer of these done than younger people. Sometimes researchers use more specialized tests that are only found in laboratories. For example, they might use tests of reaction time. This type of test measures how quickly a person can react to an event. It might involve pressing a button as soon as a light comes on, though it is usually more complicated than that. It might involve looking at a panel of four lights, waiting for one of them to be switched on, and pressing the correct button for that light as fast as possible. (There's more about reaction times and how they are tested in Chapter 3.) Older people on average are slower at these sorts of tests. What's special about these sorts of tests is that they are relatively simple. Generally speaking, people do not make any errors on these tests, especially if they are allowed to do them without time pressure. Therefore, whereas most mental tests, like memory and reasoning and so forth, can be difficult and lead to errors, these 'mental speed' tests are simple and look only at our rate of work when making very straightforward decisions. Researchers tend to use these tests as if they were telling us about some basic speed limitation of people's brains in getting through mental operations.

If Salthouse's idea is correct, the age effects on different mental abilities noted in a group of older people is caused largely by a change in general mental ability, and that change in general mental ability is due to changes in speed of information processing. Therefore, what seems like a kaleidoscope of mental change can to a great extent be explained by one simple fact: as we get older our rate of processing information in the brain slows down.

To an impressive extent Salthouse's simple idea does work. He took many researchers' data on mental abilities and age and tried out the same idea. He asked: once we remove the effects of mental speed, does age still affect general and specific mental abilities? The answer: hardly at all; when we take out the effects of mental speed on mental test scores we have removed most of the age effects too. To see what this means have another look at Figure 10. Here, we see Salthouse testing the idea that age itself does not directly affect general and specific mental abilities, even though we do know that things do change with age. Salthouse is stating that the effect of age is to slow down mental speed, that general ability declines when mental speed slows down, and that all the specific mental abilities then decline when general ability declines.

Psychologists in this type of area do try to be more specific about what they mean by mental speed. The tests they use to measure mental speed are certainly a bit more simple than the ordinary type of mental test, but they don't really tell us what is happening in the brain. Things like 'digit symbol' and 'reaction time' tests are in fact still quite complex, because we do not understand how the brain performs these tasks or how their slowing translates into changes in the biology of the brain. There the story ends, I am afraid, as far as the science goes. At this point the researchers become rather metaphorical. The favourite metaphor is the computer. Most people who have bought a computer will have been told about various aspects of its performance. One of the principal parameters is the clock speed, the processing rate of the main processor. The faster it is, the faster the computer will work and the faster it will complete complex operations. Statistical analyses that took several hours in 1990 (I used to leave my computer running overnight) now take unmeasurably small fractions of a second. So, the metaphor runs, as we grow older our brain's 'main processor' runs at a slower rate and we get the answers to mental problems more slowly, less accurately, or sometimes not at all. But a metaphor is no substitute for scientific explanation, and one necessary extension to these interesting findings is to realize the concept of 'mental' speed in terms of changes in the biology of the brain.

What research is currently going on in this area?

The study of cognitive ageing is arguably one of the most lively and exciting in the field of human intelligence – and arguably one of the most important, as the proportion of older people in the population grows larger and as people live longer and healthier lives. Indeed, about ten years ago the American Psychological Association started a new research journal called *Psychology and Aging* just to cope with the large amount of high-quality research that was taking place. Research interests are broadening in scope to ask questions such as: What are the causes of different rates of ageing of mental abilities? What are the *mechanisms* by which age impinges on mental abilities?

To follow this area up . . .

Here's the paper that my research team working on the Scottish Mental Survey 1932 published on the follow-up mental testing 66 years later.

Deary, I. J., L. J. Whalley, H. Lemmon, J. R. Crawford, & J. M. Starr (2000). The stability of individual differences in mental ability from childhood to old age: follow-up of the 1932 Scottish Mental Survey. *Intelligence*, 28, 49–55.

A popular account of this work can be found at the following website: *http://www.scre.ac.uk/rie/nl65/nl65deary.html*.

The research paper that describes the large US Department of Labor Study that looked at mental ability test scores in tens of thousands of people from young adulthood to old age is:

Avolio, B. J. & D. A. Waldman (1994). Variations in cognitive, perceptual, and psychometric abilities across the working life span: Examining the effects of race, sex, experience, education, and occupational type. *Psychology and Aging*, 9, 430–42.

And the studies that followed up people after they had been tested during world wars I and II respectively:

Owens, W. A. (1966). Age and mental abilities: A second adult follow-up. *Journal of Educational Psychology*, 57, 311–25.
Schwartzman, A. E., D. Gold, D. Andres, T. Y. Arbuckle, & J. Chaikelson (1987). Stability of intelligence: A 40 year follow-up. *Canadian Journal of Psychology*, 41, 244–56.

There are two good summaries of the Schaie's Seattle Longitudinal Study and I got much of my own information from them. The first is more accessible.

ageing

Schaie, K. W. (1994). The course of adult intellectual development. *American Psychologist*, 49, 304–13.

Schaie, K. W. (1996). *Intellectual Development in Adulthood*. Cambridge: Cambridge University Press.

The results from Salthouse's research were taken mostly from the following papers.

Salthouse, T. A. (1996a). Constraints on theories of cognitive ageing. *Psychonomic Bulletin and Review*, 3, 287–99.

Salthouse, T. A. (1996b). The processing-speed theory of adult age differences in cognition. *Psychological Review*, 103, 403–28.

The research report from which I took Figure 10 was one of the Berlin Aging Study reports:

Lindenberger, U., U. Mayr, & R. Kliegl (1993). Speed and intelligence in old age. *Psychology and Aging*, 8, 207–20.

Chapter 3
Brainy?

Why are some people cleverer than others?

What we mean when we say that some people have higher psychometric intelligence than others is that some people reliably obtain more correct answers, and often achieve these faster, on a set of mental test questions. Previously we described the patterns into which these mental test scores assort. Later we look at whether scores on mental tests are of any use in predicting things in the real world. Here we ask the following question: why do some people score better on mental test questions than others? In fact, it is a more specific question than that: what is it about the human brain that makes some people better at psychometric intelligence test items than others? And we need to be prepared for some difficulties here. What we are attempting to do in this section is ask whether there are measurable aspects of brains and brain functions that differ between people *and* that also relate to psychometric intelligence differences.

In one sense we shall address this question of the origins of intelligence differences in the next section, when the genetic and environmental contributions to intelligence are described. Just a little reflection, though, tells us that these are rather distant causes. Finding that the genetic lottery and the environmental slings and arrows influence the level of some of our mental capabilities does not tell us what it is about the brain that makes some people cleverer than others. From antiquity this question has interested commentators on the human condition.

Prior to modern-day neuroscience, the guesses at the stuff that made for the more-efficient-brain were crude and followed the fashions of the times. For over 1500 years, the ideas about the more-efficient-brain were governed by the Greek and Roman physician-philosophers who thought that the well-tempered body had to have just the right amount of the four humours, blood, phlegm, and black and yellow bile. Such early efforts occasionally alighted upon one factor that was taken up by some scientists of the 19th century – the size of the brain – but research before the later years of the 1800s really told us very little.

One of the important things to point out at the beginning of this section is that our knowledge of the brain's workings is still very incomplete. Even with the rise of the new brain sciences – neuroscience and cognitive science – we are still a long way from having a mechanistic account of how the brain thinks, emotes, and wills. Therefore, it cannot be surprising that our understanding of what makes some brains more efficient than others is still fairly rudimentary. It is possible, nevertheless, to offer some recent findings that provide intriguing clues.

For hundreds of years there have been simplistic hunches to the effect that people with greater mental powers might have brains that are bigger, faster, and/or finer-tuned. These hunches are hardly very clever; they are something that the man on the number 23 bus might have come up with given a moment or two's reflection, even without much knowledge of the brain's structure or function. Nevertheless, they have been tested and there is some scientific evidence worth recounting.

This is an area of research that I have spent some time in myself. Day in and day out I see it with its flaws and its small advances. What all of us in the research area know is that the main obstacle to progress is the lack of understanding of normal brain function and its variability. There have been great advances in understanding the brain and its functional units, but we are still a long way away from a mechanistic account of how thinking, feeling, and willing occur. The topics within this area of research that have attracted the most research effort are a rather mixed bunch. They are illustrated in Figures 11 to 14. In summary, I want to discuss how differences in psychometric intelligence relate to: brain size, the brain's electrical activity, the efficiency of visual processing, and the speed of simple reactions.

Brain size

There is a modest association between brain size and psychometric intelligence. People with bigger brains tend to have higher mental test scores. We do not know yet why this association occurs.

Figure 11 is a picture of a 65-year-old man's brain taken using a magnetic resonance imaging scanner. The man was taking part in one of my research team's studies. We have not got to the stage of publishing the data from this study yet, but this will give a clear picture of how the research is carried out. The man took a large battery of mental ability tests and gave some blood for various assessments to be made. The last part of the study involved collecting data on the size of his brain and, specifically, the sizes of some particular parts of his brain – those we considered to be involved with memory and other areas of thought. What you can see in the image is a 'slice', in which the magnetic resonance scanner has taken a picture of the contents of his head from one ear across to the other. By moving our aim further to the front and the back of his head, we collected many images and eventually we were able to get a three-dimensional view of his whole brain. With these pictures, displayed on a very high-quality computer screen, one of our team drew around the outline of the brain. That is, she carefully, without knowing anything about the man, drew an outline around all of the brain 'slices' and worked out the brain area within each slice. Note these white outlines in Figure 11. Eventually, her information was compiled to give a measure of the man's brain volume. She then repeated this procedure for 100 other men in the study. Thus, with a

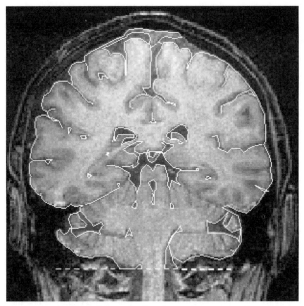

11. A picture of a living human brain taken using a magnetic resonance imaging scanner. Note the white line drawn around brain tissue to measure the area taken up by the brain in this 'slice'.

safe medical scanning machine that involves no radiation, we can now measure the size of people's brains while they are alive, and we can ask if the size of the living brain is related to intelligence test scores. Let's turn to results from other laboratories.

Nancy Andreasen is a renowned researcher into schizophrenia. Among other research, she and her team have examined the structure of the brain in people with that illness. The device her team used was a magnetic resonance imager like the one we used in our own research. Before the advent of magnetic resonance imaging, researchers had recourse to all sorts of methods that have been lampooned in the scientific and popular literature on research into intelligence. Brains were weighed after people died, skulls were filled with lead shot or other handy materials to find out how big the brain was that once resided there, and, more often, the size of the head (hat size, effectively) was measured. None of these archaic measures approaches a satisfactory way of getting at brain size (though there is a modest positive correlation between head size and brain size), but they were all born of the frustrating inability to get at brains and their sizes while people were still alive. That changed forever with the wider availability of magnetic resonance imaging machines. For the first time, the human brain was seen *in situ*, *in vivo*, in the living being. Accurate pictures of its shape and size could be reconstructed and its overall dimensions were at last available. The first person to correlate intelligence test scores with brain size – measured using magnetic resonance imaging – was the late Lee Willerman from the University of Texas at Austin. His path-breaking study in 1991 did find a modest association between brain size and cognitive ability: people with better scores on mental tests tended to have larger brains. But the study was limited by the fact that it mostly tested students, who are a rather narrow group of people with respect to their range of mental abilities. Better, then, to describe a more normal group, such as the healthy volunteers tested by Andreasen's team.

Andreasen and her team collected the largest set of data which correlated normal, healthy humans' brain sizes with their intelligence test scores. They had a broader – more normal – spread of intelligence test scores than Willerman's students, meaning that we can be more confident that these results will apply to the general population. In 1993 they examined 67 people (they are now up to about 100). These volunteers underwent a brain scan in the Mental Health Clinical Research Center at the University of Iowa. They took a standard group of mental tests, one of the Wechsler test batteries that we saw in Chapter 1. The researchers then computed a correlation between the size of the brain and the score on the mental tests. They did find a modest association, a correlation of about 0.3 to 0.4. They then asked more detailed questions about whether the size of different areas of the brain was related to people's prowess in specific types of mental ability. Results then and since are inconclusive on that issue.

Now, in psychology, people will rarely if ever believe that a finding is secure on just one or two studies. Many things can happen in a single study that can spuriously give rise to a positive result. Therefore, sensible researchers wait for many similar studies to be conducted in different, independent laboratories before they begin to accept that a finding is secure. This is certainly the case in the present topic. And so some researchers make it their work to collect all of the studies on a topic and put them together to see what the overall finding amounts to. This was done in the field of brain size and intelligence differences.

Key dataset 6

A group of researchers led by Tony Vernon gathered together all the studies up to 1999 that had examined the size of the living brain using modern brain-scanning machines and had correlated the brain volumes with the persons' scores on mental tests. Like they did, let us omit all those studies that included clinical groups (people with illnesses) and look only at healthy samples. There exist 11 such studies. Overall, that amounted to 432 people who had their brains scanned to measure the size and they all took some mental ability tests too. It is important that such an exercise of averaging across different research studies tries to find all such studies: they have to include any that showed nothing or even indicated that people scoring better on cognitive tests had smaller brains (there are none). That done, the average correlation was about 0.4. That is a moderate effect size: not a huge association, but large enough to state securely that people who score better on mental tests do tend to have bigger brains.

To the best that we can judge, then, the untutored guess that the cleverer person is literally more 'brainy' has some modest force. The finding is fascinating more in what it does not tell us than in what it does. The relationship between the size of the brain and better scores on cognitive tests begs for some explanation, some mechanistic account. It is fair to say that the best anyone has at present is yet more guesses. Some have suggested that the bigger brains have more nerve cells. Some suggest that the nerve cells are the same in number, but they have more connections in the bigger brain. Others have come up with the idea that the bigger brain comes about because cleverer people have thicker fatty layers surrounding the nerve cells; these 'myelin sheaths' are the electrical insulation that surround nerve cells' cables and help them to send messages more quickly. There are other suggestions, but they are all speculative. The work of the next decades in this field will be to find out why this brain size – cognitive ability association occurs.

The brain's electrical activity

The evidence is mixed, but there is some indication that the brain's electrical responses show differences between people of different levels of intelligence. People with higher intelligence, on average, appear to elicit faster, more complex, and differently shaped electrical responses. The main problem in this line of research is that, of the 100+ studies available to date, hardly one exactly repeats the previous studies, so we do not have a check on the trustworthiness of the findings.

Have a look at Figure 12. It is a trace of the electrical activity of the human brain. (In fact, it is an average of one person's brain's activity over many encounters with the same stimulus, as I shall explain below.) Going along the bottom of the Figure from left to right, the time span is about half a second (500 milliseconds). Going from bottom to top, we are measuring electrical activity in just a few millionths of a volt. The nerve cells of the brain transmit messages along their lengths by electrical discharge. Also, the chemical messages that one nerve cell sends to the next make alterations to the electrical status of the brain's

49

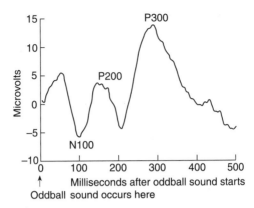

12. A graph of the brain's electrical activity. This is an average of one person's brain's activity to a number of 'oddball' stimuli.

cells. As long as we are alive – alert, awake, asleep, whatever – our brain is electrically active and this activity can be measured using very sensitive equipment to give a picture, the electroencephalogram (or EEG). For example, we know that the brain's electrical activity is faster when we are doing mental arithmetic than when we are relaxing.

A big advance was made in this area over 30 years ago when psychologists first became able to measure the brain's electrical activity in response to simple, discrete stimuli. The EEG activity mentioned above is an amalgam of all that is psychologically happening to us at any one time. If we tried to get people to perform a small, specific psychological act and we then look at the EEG we would learn nothing, because the small amount of the brain's electrical activity that was related to that single act would be swamped by the rest of the activity. It would be like trying to hear a distant skylark's song standing beside the M1 during the rush hour. Researchers hit on the idea of teasing out the tiny electrical response to simple mental acts.

First let's discuss their approach. They test people in a quiet laboratory, where sounds and other distractions are minimized. With their subjects sitting comfortably, they record the electrical activity of the brain by placing some small, metal electrodes on the surface of the scalp. The person being tested would, for example, listen to a long series – perhaps hundreds – of tones, just simple sounds. Most of these sounds, which occur every few seconds, are the same. However, the occasional one is different, perhaps much lower in pitch. These occasional different tones which break up the stream of repetitive normal sounds are called 'oddball' tones, because they are different from the norm. The experimenter asks the person to listen out for the occasional 'oddball' tones, perhaps to count them just to make sure they paid attention. The experiment keeps going until over 50 or even 100 oddballs have been heard. The experimenter saves all the brain's electrical responses to each of the oddball sounds and keeps a separate store of the brain's responses to every one of the normal tones. Now, any one of the oddball's electrical responses is a chaotic-looking squiggly line. If you looked at all 50 or 100 of the squiggly lines representing the brain's electrical response to each of the various oddball sounds, they would all look different. However, hidden within each one of the responses is a very small, fairly constant 'signal', which is the brain's specific response to the oddball sound. By averaging all the squiggly lines one can take out the EEG that was nothing to do with the oddball and just leave the oddball-related electrical activity. This is because the electrical response to the oddball sound is the only 'constant' pattern in the dozens of responses; it emerges intact when the rest of the chaos averages to a flat line. It's then that you get a wavy line like that shown in Figure 12: an average of how the brain responds, electrically, to a sound that is different from other sounds in a stream of simple tones. This average electrical activity of the brain to a stimulus is called the 'event related potential' or ERP. Its shape has characteristic peaks and troughs.

The arrow in Figure 12 indicates when the stimulus – the oddball sound – came on. Note too that, after about $\frac{1}{3}$ of a second (at 300 milliseconds) there is an especially large positive wave (upward-going) of electrical activity. I have labelled this P300. It is called the P300 for the following reasons: 'P' because it is electrically positive and '300' because it occurs about 300 milliseconds after the stimulus which elicits it. The P300 occurs in response to the oddball sound only, not to the normal tones. It is thought to reflect brain activity related to noticing difference or novelty. In most humans it typically, as we see here, occurs about $\frac{3}{10}$ of a second after the oddball sound starts. There is an earlier positive peak, labelled P200. (This earlier positive peak is discussed further below.) In the person whose responses I used for Figure 12 you can see that the 'P200' occurs a bit earlier than 200 milliseconds after the oddball sound. There is an even earlier negative electrical trough, called N100: a negative electrical wave at $\frac{1}{10}$ of a second (100 milliseconds) after the oddball sound comes on. So, when the brain notices even small stimuli and makes decisions about them, we get predictable types and patterns of electrical responses from our brains. For the oddball sound, the N100, P200, and P300 are typical electrical events. Other types of event have their own characteristic waves. These diagrams, then, can tell us about how fast and vigorously the brain responds on average to events in the outside world, and they reflect the decisions we have to make about these events.

Almost as soon as researchers were able to collect these diagrams of brain responses, some asked about individual differences between people. That is, they noticed that the peaks of the waves in the panel occurred after a shorter time in some people than in others. In some, the peaks were taller than in others. Perhaps brighter people, then, had a faster brain? Perhaps their electrical responses to events were that bit faster than people with lower intelligence test scores? Before going into that possibility and some others, it's useful to inform you that my colleague Peter Caryl and I tried twice during the 1990s to read and assess all research studies ever reported in the scientific journals that looked at psychometric intelligence and the brain's electrical responses. What we found and reported to the research community was, frankly, a mess. It's probably fairly obvious that these types of study are technically difficult to set up. They need specialized equipment and there are many different ways they can be done. The problem was that we found hardly any studies that repeated the same procedures, so it was hard to draw out any well-attested, replicated results. We did, though, find some hints at regularities in the research. I would stress that these are indications only: none of them is certain, but all are interesting possibilities for making some links between the brain's activity and the scores on intelligence tests.

First, *the timing of the peaks and troughs of the electrical response*. Some researchers got the idea that cleverer people had a faster brain electrical response to simple stimuli. There does seem to be some evidence that these occur some thousandths of a second earlier in people with higher psychometric intelligence. So, if the trace shown in Figure 12 was an average person, a brighter person might, on average, have their electrical peaks occur a bit to the left. The largest focus of research here has been the timing of the P300 wave peak, which might appear at a bit less than 300 milliseconds in higher intelligence test scorers, and a bit more in lower scorers.

Second, *the overall complexity of the electrical response*. Some researchers got the idea that brighter people had a more consistent brain electrical response to stimuli. Therefore, all of the 50 or 100 or so electrical responses to, say, an oddball tone would be very alike in a person with high intelligence. When averaged up, they should retain much of the complexity of the originals. On the other hand, people with lower mental test scores were thought, perhaps, to have more variable electrical responses. Therefore, when their responses were averaged, a cruder, less detailed waveform resulted. Quite a few research teams have tried to test this idea – that on average brighter people have a more complex brain response and less bright people have a simpler-looking response. It even has a popular name, the 'string length measure' – if one laid a string over a more complex (more squiggly) electrical response, then it would be longer than if one laid a piece over a simpler response. The result? Hard to tell. Some studies suggest that this idea does work and some that it doesn't. Researchers are trying at present to find out why this discrepancy exists.

Third, *the shape of some selected parts of the electrical response*. Some researchers got the idea that more intelligent people had a differently shaped brain electrical response to simple stimuli. Again, take a look at Figure 12. Notice a large kink in the trace, from N100 to P200, where the electrical voltage swings from negative (going down) to quite a high positive value. That excursion happens between about $\frac{1}{7}$ and $\frac{1}{5}$ of a second after the event – that is, after the oddball sound (or whatever) occurred. We think that this electrical activity is something to do with our attempts to tell one thing from another, in making a simple discrimination. It's been noticed that some people have steeper swings in this part of the electrical response than others. In other words, the slope that climbs from N100 up to P200 is steep in some people and flatter in others. And it seems to be the case that, on average, people who score better on intelligence tests have steeper slopes in this part of the brain's electrical response to simple events. This statement is based on just a few studies, and the results require exploring in more and bigger groups of people.

The efficiency of visual processing

There is a well-established, moderate association between the efficiency of the early stages of visual perception and intelligence test scores.

Think of the situation where you enter a dark room, put on a light briefly, and then switch it off again. For a short time after returning to darkness you have an image of things in the room, a fleeting, fast-dissolving 'shot' of the scene. That very brief access to visual information after the actual stimulus has been taken away is called our iconic memory and it lasts just a fraction of a second. Next think of the situation where you are watching the television and something – an image or a word perhaps – flashes up on the screen very quickly and then disappears. Pop music videos are common culprits in producing this sort of event. In a group of people, some people will catch the information and some will not. It will have come and gone too fast for some and not for others, even if everyone attended closely. Therefore, there might be individual differences in how efficiently people extract information from iconic memory, and researchers, including me, have asked whether this relates to intelligence differences. The test we use most often is called inspection time.

Look at Figure 13a. Notice the simple shapes with two vertical lines that are joined at the top. One of the vertical lines is longer then the other. In one of the images the long line is on the left and in the other the long line is on the right. When you look at each image you'll find it very easy to tell whether the long line is on the right or the left because there is a large difference in the lengths of the lines. These two simple shapes are the stimuli we use in inspection time tests. What we do in this test is randomly present *one or the other* of these two shapes to a subject and

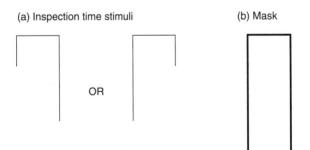

(a) Inspection time stimuli   (b) Mask

OR

13. (a) The stimulus materials used in the inspection time test that measures people's ability to process visual information quickly. (b) The stimulus is followed by a 'masking' figure that has thick lines of equal lengths.

ask them to tell us whether the long line was on the right or the left. Now, the immediate problem you will see with this test is that everyone will get all of the answers correct, because the question is very easy. There are two ways used to make it harder. First we can flash one or other shape to the person for a short amount of time, measured in thousandths of a second. If it is presented before the eyes only fleetingly, it is harder to tell where the long line was. Also, immediately after the shape is shown, we can remove it and replace it with another type of image, something to 'wipe' the impression of the figure from the eye and its brain. This second, interfering image is called a 'mask' and one type of mask is shown in Figure 13b. It has thicker lines and the lines are the same length.

Let's look in detail at what happens to a person taking part in an inspection time test. Usually they sit in a quiet, dim room in a psychology laboratory. They look at a screen that is about 50 cm away – this might be a computer screen, or a panel of light-emitting diode lights, or a screen on some special device. They get a brief warning that something is about to happen, usually a little cross-hair or a dot on the screen. One of the two shapes at random from the section (a) of Figure 13 appears on the screen only briefly. After the figure is taken away, the experimenter replaces it with the masking shape (shown in Figure 13b). The person tells the experimenter whether the long line was on the left or the right. The experimenter records whether that answer was correct or wrong. Now, it is especially important to appreciate that the person giving the answers does not have to answer quickly or within a given time. The experimenter only needs to know whether or not the person is correct, not how fast they responded.

The test is repeated, sometimes hundreds of times. About half of the time the long line is on the right and half on the left, but it is not possible to predict the order. The shapes are shown for varying lengths of time. Sometimes the shape is shown for a long time, for example a quarter of a second. Almost no one will make errors when they see the stimulus for that length of time. Sometimes the shape appears for just a few thousandths of a second. In that case, no one will be able to 'see' the stimulus at better than chance level. (Note that even just guessing will get the correct answer 50% of the time.)

What we find in this test is that, as the two-line shape is presented for longer times, the person is more likely to be correct in identifying the position of the long line. But we also find striking differences between people in how well they do on this simple inspection time test. Some people can report the position of the long line accurately even when it is shown only briefly, whereas others are guessing at no better than chance at the same duration. Therefore, researchers wondered whether there was a relation between this simple aspect of the efficiency of visual perception and intelligence test scores. The first studies of this type were done in the mid-1970s by Ted Nettelbeck and his colleagues at the University of Adelaide, and to date there have been dozens of other studies, involving many hundreds of people in four continents. The overall answer is yes, there is a moderate association between how good people are at the inspection time test and how well they score on intelligence tests. The correlation is about 0.4. People with higher intelligence test scores seem on average to be more efficient in processing visual information when it is presented only briefly. They can accurately tell what has been shown to them when others see only a blur. Therefore, this test of the efficiency of processing simple visual information relates to human intelligence differences.

How much does that tell us about what it means to be clever, at least as defined by a score on intelligence tests? Some researchers say it tells us quite a lot and some say it tells us not very much. Some take the view that the inspection time test is a simple function, an indicator of some basic limitation in the brain's ability to cope with incoming information. They have even compared it to the clock speed of a computer: that is, the people with the better inspection times have been likened to computers with faster clock speeds. They go about the world taking in and chewing up information at a faster rate than others. There is support for this view from various sources. People's inspection time slows as they get older. There are studies of illnesses and chemical compounds that slow down inspection time; and these factors also seem to affect psychometric intelligence. So, maybe, then, one smallish contribution to being brighter is having a brain that can process simple information rather quickly. This would agree with the old adage that people who are brighter are 'quick on the uptake'. Essentially, the more intelligent person might be able to sample the world faster, making distinctions that go by too quickly for others.

But it is only fair to tell you that there are other views. Those who read the research reports firmly accept that there is an association between inspection time and intelligence, but some psychologists explain this in a different way. They say there could be other reasons for brighter people doing well on inspection time tests – it might have nothing to do with how fast their brain processes information. It could be that more intelligent people are more motivated or more relaxed or quicker to learn any task. Therefore, inspection time might be just another thing they do well because they try harder, or they don't get so nervous in the lab, or they pick up the idea of the task better and quicker. If any of these ideas were true, it would be the case that inspection time was really acting just like an intelligence test, and not testing something basic about the brain. Another view is that people with better intelligence test scores might find some trick or strategy for doing the inspection time test better. Even though the task is meant to be a simple one that everyone does in the same way, the brighter person might pick up some strategy that gets them a better score: nothing, then, to do with how fast they process simple visual information. For example, some people can spot a small apparent movement after the two-lines figure is removed (with the best equipment this does not happen), and they try to use that to make better decisions. It would be fair to say that there have been some (but not enough) attempts to test the alternative ideas I have outlined in this paragraph and that there is not much evidence – if any at all – to support them.

Two views, then, about why people's inspection time differences have a moderate association with intelligence test scores. (1) It's because the less intelligent person's brain processes information at a slower rate on average. In this view, inspection time would be a *cause* of intelligence differences; just one among others, obviously, but this would be an important finding. (2) It's because inspection time is essentially just another test that bright people find a way to do relatively well. In this view, inspection time would be merely a *symptom* or *consequence* of intelligence differences. Who's right? We do not know for certain. On balance, there is little evidence for the latter view, but that's partly because these ideas are vague and hard to test in experiments. At present it is worth keeping open the possibility that we have discovered a way of testing some important limitation of the brain's ability to make discriminations and decisions. It is exciting to have found psychometric test scores relating to something that at least looks very simple. Researchers need to do more digging to find what it is about the brain that causes these differences between people in their ability to cope with simple information.

Reaction time

People with higher intelligence test scores have, on average, shorter and less variable reaction times.

Look at Figure 14, which shows a box that measures people's reaction times. First, let's describe the equipment and how it is used by experimenters. Recall that inspection time was intended to assess how well people could make a discrimination when the visual figure was shown for only a very brief time. It was to do with speed of taking in visual information from the world. There was absolutely no need to respond quickly. Reaction time, on the other hand, is to do with how

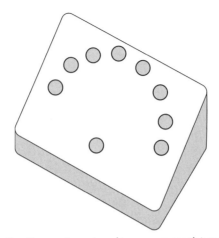

14. The reaction time equipment used to measure people's reaction times, decision times, and movement times.

quickly people can make a correct physical response to a signal. The box shown in Figure 14 has eight buttons arranged in a semi-circle. At the bottom of the box there is one other button, equal in distance from the other eight. This separate button is called the 'home' button and the other eight are called 'target' buttons. Each button contains a light and is also a press-down switch.

Here's the sequence of events when someone is having their reaction time measured. The person being tested places their preferred finger on the home button. One of the eight buttons in the semi-circle around the home button lights up. The person, as quickly as possible, lifts their finger off the home button and presses the target button that lit up. The process is repeated dozens or more times.

Here's how the person's reaction time gets measured in that simple event. When the target light comes on a timer starts immediately. The timer only gets switched off when the person being tested presses the target button down. The time that lapsed from the target light being turned on until the person pressed down the target button is the person's reaction time. As a general guide, the time this sort of reaction takes ranges in different people from under $\frac{1}{2}$ a second to about $\frac{3}{4}$ of a second. Because not every single reaction is identical, the dozens that are collected by the experimenter are used to calculate an average for that person. But note that all those separate reactions can tell us something else, apart from the average. Some people are relatively consistent: their individual reaction times are all about the same, falling into a small range of values. Other people are more variable, with quite a wide spread of faster and slower reactions. Therefore, we can measure how fast a person can react on average and we can also measure how variable/consistent they are in their reactions.

Before we proceed to look at how well reaction time relates to intelligence test scores, I need to add a few more details to the reaction time test. First, note that in the situation I described the person was reacting to one out of eight lights. Because they have to press the correct button out of eight, they have to make a choice of which is the correct light, and so this procedure is called *choice reaction time*. The choices can be any number, though two, four, and eight are the most commonly used in the choice reaction time procedure. When there is only one target button – imagine the box in Figure 14 with just the home button and one target button – the person just waits for the light to come on and responds to it. In that case, there is no choice to be made and the procedure is called *simple reaction time*.

Choice reaction time and simple reaction time form the basis of many different procedures in psychology. There have been measures of reaction time since the mid-19th century. There was some faltering interest around the start of the 20th century in whether reaction times, because they seemed so basic, were related to intelligence test score differences. But the work really began in earnest in the late 1970s and early 1980s when a type of psychology called 'cognitive' psychology came into vogue and began to study the timing of human mental processes. Since then dozens of studies, involving in total thousands of subjects, have looked at the association between reaction time and intelligence test scores. The researcher who brought reaction time to the study of intelligence and did much of this work is Arthur Jensen from the University of California at Berkeley. The finding: there is a small but consistent association between speed in simple and choice reaction time experiments and psychometric intelligence. The correlation is often about 0.2 or a bit higher. People with better intelligence test scores are, on average, faster in their reactions. Also, just as consistent a finding is that people with better intelligence test scores are more consistent in their reaction times. People who don't score so well on intelligence tests have, then, slower and more variable reactions on average.

Again, as we noted with the inspection time findings, it is really quite exciting to find that something as complex as an intelligence test score can be related to something as simple as reaction time. However, it would be reductive to think that intelligence is about faster and more consistent reactions. The association, though consistent, is not large and only a small portion of intelligence differences at best could ever be explained by reaction time's speed and variability differences.

Again, as we found with inspection time, although most researchers acknowledge that the association between reaction times and intelligence is a real advance, they disagree strongly about what the connection means. Some psychologists, again, think it is an indicator that the person with higher intelligence has a brain that is a faster and more consistent processor of information. That is, they assume that the simple procedure involved in reaction time can tell us about some basic limitations or operating characteristics of the brain. On the other hand, those who dissent from this view say that reaction time is in fact rather complex and can be affected by some of the things that affect our performance on intelligence tests. Really, this is mostly a replay of the argument current within the inspection time researches – that is, whether speed in reaction time is a *cause* or merely a *symptom* of intelligence differences.

There is one possible reason for the association between reaction times and intelligence test scores that will have occurred to some and that needs countering. It would be easy to assume that the association between reaction times and intelligence comes about because reaction time involves working quickly and accurately and so does performing on intelligence tests. But, in fact, the association between reaction time and psychometric intelligence tests is found also with those intelligence tests that are not speeded, where people are left to take as long as they like to complete the questions.

One more bit of detail on reaction times. Have another look at the reaction time box drawn in Figure 14. If you think about the activity of completing a single reaction time trial you can imagine the sorts of mental processes you go through. Attend to the target buttons; notice which one has been lit; lift finger from the home button; get to the lit target light and press it as fast as possible. This involves a combination of decision-making and reacting. Some psychologists have been keen to separate the thinking and doing parts of reaction times, and this is how they did it. Instead of having a single timer in the box, they have two, to give a measure of the person's 'decision time' and their 'movement time'. Here's how.

As before, the task is a choice reaction time test with all eight of the semi-circle's buttons being possible targets. The person puts their preferred finger on the home button. Gets ready. Attends to the target lights. One of the target lights comes on and the first timer starts. The clock is ticking ready to measure the speed of the person's response. Here's the difference. This time, the first clock stops when the person's finger is lifted from the home button: that is, the first timer calculates how long it took the person to decide to lift their finger and make a start toward the target button after the target light came on. This first time is the person's 'decision time'. As soon as the first timer stops, the second one begins – that is, when the person takes their finger off the home button. It stops again when they put their finger on the target button. This second timer calculates the time between the finger coming off the home button and going on to the target: that is, it is measuring the time it took the person to *move* from the home button, having *decided* which button was correct. This is called the person's 'movement time'. Thus reaction time can be split into decision and movement sections and measured separately: both the speed and the variability of the decision time and the movement time can also be assessed. It's a surprise to many people that the decision time takes about $\frac{1}{3}$ of a second and that the movement time is much less, about only $\frac{1}{6}$ of a second. That is, it takes almost twice as long to lift the finger off the home button as it does to go from the home button to the target.

Both decision time and movement time relate to intelligence test scores. People with higher intelligence test scores have faster decision and movement times. With regard to variability, it tends to be the variability of only the decision time that relates to intelligence – people with better intelligence test scores are less variable in their decision times – whereas there is no relation with variability of movement time.

What research is currently going on in this area?

One idea that ties up a lot of this field is that brighter people have a faster 'mental speed'. This broad idea, that cleverer people are somehow mentally faster, is an old and vague one. I can certainly trace it back at least as far as the 17th-century English philosopher Thomas Hobbes, and it has never really gone out of fashion. Psychologists today often refer to the 'mental speed' or 'information processing speed' 'theory' of intelligence. What they mean by that is that people who score better on intelligence tests might in part be cleverer because some key aspect(s) of the brain proceeds faster. My principal problem with this overall idea is that my colleagues can't make up their mind how to measure this mental speed. Some use reaction times. Some use inspection times. Some use the brain's electrical responses. Some even measure how long it takes electrical impulses to travel along people's nerves. But these are all different measures, and it is an odd theory that can be tested without a common yardstick, and some of these mental speed 'yardsticks' don't relate to each other very well at all. The truth is that we do not have an agreed measure of how fast the brain processes information, and that is because the workings of the nerve cells and their networks are largely mysterious. We must summarize by concluding, therefore, that intelligence is related to many things that involve speed of processing information, but that scientists have difficulty in conceptualizing 'mental speed' in a uniform way. I think it is likely that that will change quite quickly with new methods of brain scanning. At present, though, we need to acknowledge what findings there are. Those described above are real and interesting, but their limitations must be acknowledged.

There are more and more studies of brain size and intelligence appearing nowadays; in normal adults, in children, in old people, and in groups of people with illnesses. The focus is moving on from just finding out yet again that bigger brains tend to go with higher intelligence. The search is on for the explanation. Researchers are beginning to examine the way that people's brains cope with the inspection time task by having them perform it in brain scanners and watching the activity in different parts of the brain as they do the test. There are more studies appearing of how drugs that affect the brain also affect inspection time, reaction times, and mental test performance. There are studies coming out on how ageing affects the speed of processing of information (see Chapter 2).

To follow this area up . . .

This was the one chapter in the present book for which I was not able to pull out a few key sources and describe them in more detail. A research colleague from my own department and I wrote a short, general overview of biologically oriented approaches to intelligence as follows.

Deary, I. J. & P. G. Caryl (1997). Neuroscience and human intelligence differences. *Trends in Neurosciences*, 20, 365–71.

The best sources for follow-up material are the chapters by Tony Vernon, Ian Deary, and David Lohman in the following book:

Robert J. Sternberg (ed.) (2000). *Handbook of Intelligence*. Cambridge: Cambridge University Press.

My own recent monograph on this area is aimed at fellow researchers and students and is thus technical rather than popular in style.

Deary, I. J. (2000). *Looking Down on Human Intelligence: From Psychometrics to the Brain*. Oxford: Oxford University Press.

Here's the article in which Nancy Andreasen first reported the association between *in vivo* brain size and intelligence in normal people.

Andreasen, N.C. (et al.) (1993). Intelligence and brain structure in normal individuals. *American Journal of Psychiatry*, 150, 130–4.

Here's a review of the inspection time research that I wrote for the non-specialist reader.

Deary, I. J. & C. Stough (1996). Intelligence and inspection time: achievements, prospects and problems. *American Psychologist*, 51, 599–608.

Chapter 4

'They f—— you up, your mum and dad' (Larkin)

Are intelligence differences a result of genes or environments or both?

Most people who are curious about human intelligence want to know whether there is much information about its origins: do genes have an appreciable effect?; what is the impact of the environment? Let's start with a simple result: people in the same family tend to be more alike in their intelligence test scores than unrelated individuals. Like many other human characteristics, being clever tends to run in families. And the closer the family relation in an extended family, the closer is the resemblance in intelligence level. However, that is a near-useless finding because it cannot possibly tell us the origins of the contributions to intelligence: we share an environment, as well as genes, with our parents. Perhaps the environment they provided – the nutrition, the books, the schooling, the encouragement, the health care, the not smoking, and so forth – helped shape our intellectual capabilities? Maybe. But maybe it was the genes they gave us, the 50% of our genes that we share with our mothers and the 50% with our fathers. We can't pull these two effects apart. The same people who mixed up our genetic cocktail also produced the environment. How can we find a way to study the effects of each separately?

Research in this area focuses on the study of twins and the study of people who are adopted. Sometimes in this area twins are called 'experiments of nature' and people who are adopted are called 'experiments of society'. In what comes next I want to explain how these groups can help us to understand the origins of human intelligence differences.

Key dataset 7

Twins

Everyone knows that there are two types of twins: identical and non-identical. The key thing for researchers is that identical twins have exactly the same genes. What happens is that a sperm from the father fertilizes an egg from the mother and creates an embryo. At a very early stage the embryo splits into two. Therefore, what might have been one being becomes two genetically identical beings. Non-identical twins are only as genetically alike as any brother or sister. They have on average 50% of their genes in common. What happens is that two sperm from the father fertilize two eggs from the mother, creating two separate embryos, which develop into two genetically non-identical human beings. So, identical twins have 100% of their genes in common and non-identical twins only 50%. Therefore, we have a remarkable natural occurrence whereby we have types of people whom we know are always the same age and are either genetically identical or share 50% of their genes.

Now look at Figure 15. This refers to a pair of identical twins brought up in the same family. There is a box each for twin 1 and twin 2 of the pair. Since they are identical twins, they have to be the same sex, so twin 1

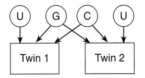

15. A diagram of the environmental and genetic influences on intelligence for *identical twins reared together*.

might be John Smith and twin 2 might be James Smith. The boxes just represent the twins and something about them that interests us, such as their score on an intelligence test. The first box, then, could be John Smith's intelligence test score and the second could be James Smith's intelligence test score. So we have two intelligence test scores from our two identical twins. Next we want to think about the influences on those test scores, specifically the influences of environment and of genes, and we want to ask which of these influences are shared by John and James Smith and which are not.

In the Figure, note the label G and that there is an arrow pointing from it to both of the twins of the identical twin pair. G stands for genes, and the arrow pointing to each of the twins from the same G captures the fact that they have identical genes. Now look at Figure 16, which refers to non-identical twins brought up together in the same family. Again G represents the effects of genes on measured intelligence, but notice the difference between this and Figure 15. Here there are two different circles with Gs in them to signify that the genes of these two twins are not identical. However, we do know that non-identical twins share half of their genes on average. So we can join their sources of genes with an arrow labelled $\frac{1}{2}$ to indicate this.

Before going into more detail on this, it is worth focusing in general on the environment and how it might be partitioned. Anyone brought up

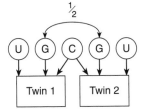

16. A diagram of the environmental and genetic influences on intelligence for *non-identical twins reared together*.

with brothers and/or sisters has two separable aspects to their environment. There are those aspects of the environment that they share with their brothers and sisters. For example, they might share feeding patterns and diets, family outings and holidays, the home's books and other educational resources, the parents' attitudes, and so forth. Then there are those aspects of the environment that are their experiences alone. They might have had different illnesses, have different friends, read different books, have different hobbies, even experience the 'same' events very differently, and so forth. Therefore, when we think about the environment we need to be more specific. It can at least be divided into that which we have in common with our siblings and that which we have to ourselves, our shared and private experiences. The environmental effects we share with our siblings are called the common (C) environment. (It is also called 'shared' or 'between-family' environment in the research literature.) The environmental effects we do not share with our siblings are called the unique (U) environment. (This is sometimes referred to as 'unshared' or 'within-family' environment.) To recap. When we ask about the effects of the environment on intelligence – or anything else – we can be more specific and ask if it was our *family upbringing* that had the effect and/or our *unique experiences* that we did not share even with members of our close family.

Back to Figures 15 and 16. In both, C and U are experienced in the same way by each member of any twin pair – identical or non-identical – brought up in the same home. They share a common environment

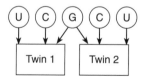

17. A diagram of the environmental and genetic influences on intelligence for *identical twins reared apart*.

(denoted by a single C with two arrows): being a member of a particular family will produce an effect of the environment that they share. There are separate U circles for each member of each twin pair. This represents the fact that they have some non-shared aspects of their environment that can affect their level of intelligence.

Let's recap. If we ask about the influences on the intelligence of the identical twins reared together, we see three sources: genes, which they share 100%; common environment, which they share 100%; and unshared environment, which they don't share at all. For the non-identical twins reared together: genes, which they share 50%; common environment, which they share 100%; and unshared environment, which they don't share at all.

Next, let's look at twins (identical and non-identical) who have been separated very early in life and have been brought up in completely different families. This is a rare occurrence, so there are not many studies on it around the world. In situations where it does happen, it is extremely difficult to trace and test the twins involved. Figure 17 shows a pair of identical twins reared apart. The two twins in such a situation still have 100% of genes in common. They will still have a portion of the environment that they share with other members of the rearing family, and they have their unique experiences too. However, *they have no 'shared' environment with their twin* because they were separated from them to be brought up in different families. So, unlike Figure 15, Figure 17 has two different C circles, one for each identical twin.

In summary, for identical twins reared apart, the influences on their intelligence test scores may be summed up as follows. There are genetic influences, which they share 100%; there are aspects of the environment that they share with the siblings in the rearing family, which they share *not at all* with their twin; and there are aspects of the environment that are unique to themselves.

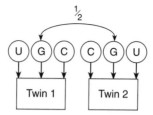

18. A diagram of the environmental and genetic influences on intelligence for *non-identical twins reared apart*.

Figure 18 pertains to non-identical twins reared apart. As with the identical twins reared in different families, these non-identical twins have no 'shared' environment with each other. Therefore, we can summarize the contributions to their intelligence test scores as follows: genes, which they share 50%; 'common' environment which they *don't share at all* with their twin; and unique environment which of course they don't share at all.

The most recent and best-known dataset of this type is the Minnesota Study of Twins Reared Apart (MISTRA). In the Minnesota Centre for Twin and Adoption Research (MICTAR), Tom Bouchard and his colleagues have the privilege of bringing together from all over the world the MISTRA twins (identical and non-identical) – and some triplets – who were separated during childhood and typically for most of their lives until that point. For a week in the MICTAR they are taken through 50 hours of psychological and medical tests and questionnaires. Their physical state, abilities, personalities, work patterns, and personal lives are documented as fully as the time allows.

The human interest in the study alone is astonishing. Bringing twins or triplets together after they have spent most of their lives apart is something that appeals to our emotions and curiosity. Tom Bouchard communicates that side of things very well. He has pictures of two male identical twins who were both firemen and who looked identical despite

19. One of the pairs of twins taking part in the Minnesota Study of Twins Reared Apart.

not having spent their lives together (Figure 19). Here's the report of Gerald Levy's and Mark Newman's meeting. "Both sport sideburns and moustaches of equal length and with similar curl, both wear metal-frame aviator-type eyeglasses. Their mannerisms are alike, their voices indistinguishable, their gaits identical." Says Newman: "Every time we did something it seemed to be in unison. That's when it really started to get scary." But I don't want to focus on the anecdotal side of the study, because the hard psychological facts themselves are just as astonishing.

Among all these tests, one of the areas of function that is examined most scrupulously is mental ability. Each pair of twins gets a large set of cognitive ability, intelligence-style tests. Then the researchers correlate the test scores to discover whether one member of a twin pair tends to get the same score as the other member. Among the tests they receive is the full Wechsler Adult Intelligence Scales, an earlier version of the one that we met in Chapter 1. It takes about an hour and a half or more to administer, with a different examiner testing each member of the twin pair. How similar are pairs of identical twins who lived apart for most of their lives? Well, their total scores on the Wechsler battery of mental tests correlate at 0.69. This is a very high correlation and not that much different from pairs of identical twins who have spent their

73

lives together and whose scores correlate at 0.88. For some other mental ability tests, the correlations from the Minnesota study were the same for the identical twins who were reared together and apart. For example, Raven's Progressive Matrices is reckoned to be one of the best single tests of the general factor in human intelligence. The correlation of Raven's test scores (with a vocabulary scale score added to it) for reared-apart identical twins was 0.78. For reared-together identical twins it was 0.76.

That's the principal and surprising result. Identical twin pairs who spent their lives apart end up just about as similar in intelligence as those who spent their lives together.

Later we'll look at whether the results of the Minnesota study could be due to things other than genetic similarity. For now, though, we must fully appreciate their near-incredible conclusions. The results indicate that, on intelligence, identical twins who have lived separate lives are almost as alike on intelligence test scores as identical twins who lived shared lives. Look back again at Figures 15 and 17, concerning identical twins reared together and apart. The things that tend to make members of a twin pair similar are the circles that have two arrows emitting from them. The 'apart' twins share only genes. The 'together' twins share genes and common (family) environment. What can we conclude, then, if we find that the 'apart' and 'together' twins are just about as alike on intelligence? The conclusion is that the C factor, common environment, has a negligible effect. Both types of twin pair share only the fact that they have identical genes, so the genes seem to be important. A counter-intuitive and rather unpalatable finding to assiduous parents: that family upbringing has very little effect on intelligence level. Most of us would begin with the opposite assumption.

Let's just drive home how similar identical twins are even when they have lived apart for most of their lives. Look at Figure 20. (Don't bother

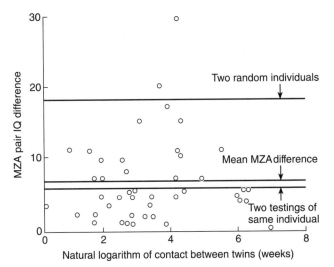

20. A diagram to show the similarity of IQ scores in identical twins reared apart (MZA). It also shows that there was no correlation between time spent together and similarity in IQ scores.

about the details in the graph at the moment. We shall come to that in a minute or two.) For now, just look at the numbers that run vertically up the side. They are IQ score differences: 10, 20, 30 points, and so on. Notice the top horizontal line. It occurs at about an IQ difference of 18. It's the average difference between two people picked at random off the street.

Now let's take the opposite extreme. I give a mental ability test to people and then test them all once again. I want to compare how the same person scores when tested twice. Now, each person won't get exactly the same score. We'll find that there is a bit of wobble. Some might be a bit sharper on one day than the other, might be more distracted, might just have had a cup of coffee, might be thinking about a fight they had at home that morning, and so on through the complexities of human conscious thought. We are not totally reliable

75

machines and mental ability tests will not always register the same score on the same person. (If we took their temperature or their blood pressure we would not get exactly the same result when we tested them twice either.) The average amount of wobble for the same person is about 5 or so IQ points, and you can see that horizontal line drawn along Figure 20. It's marked as 'two testings of the same individual.'

We are now set to answer the key question. How alike are identical twins reared apart – people with the same genes but brought up in different environments? If the family environment is all-important and they have not shared it with their twin, then they might be as alike as our two hypothetical random strangers. If genes are more important they might be more like the same person tested twice. Have a look at Figure 20 again. The answer is the horizontal line marked 'mean MZA difference' (identical ['monozygotic'] twins reared apart). It's only marginally higher than the same person tested twice. Identical twins reared apart are very similar in intelligence.

All we know so far is that this remarkable study of twins reared apart has told us that identical twins who do not spent their lives in contact with each other turn out to have highly similar levels of intelligence – nearly as similar as the same person tested twice. Some of what we know points to that similarity being caused substantially by genetic similarity, but we can think of other possibilities too. In fact, three things come to mind straight away.

1   The twins spent time together in their mother's womb.
2   Members of each twin pair might have been placed in very similar homes, even though they were separated in early life. Whoever arranged the adoptions might, with humane intent, try to arrange such a state of affairs. Therefore, the separated twins might have lived in very similar environments even though they did not spend their time in contact with each other.
3   Not all of these 'separated' twins were separated for *all* of their lives

before they were united via the MISTRA to take their intelligence tests. Some had spent some childhood together and some had adult contact. So, again, there was some opportunity to share environmental influences that might have made their intelligence levels similar.

Bouchard and his team tried to look at the latter two of these possibilities. They looked at the similarities of the families and homes into which individuals from each separated twin pair were placed. They made estimates of the adopted parents' social class, of the facilities in the family homes, and of the more psychological aspects of the family environment. Some of these family-related things did associate moderately strongly across twin pairs. Some of these aspects related weakly to intelligence level. But the conclusion was that the effect of being placed in similar environments made only a tiny contribution to the intellectual similarity of the identical twins reared apart. The main influence seemed still to be the genes.

Next, the team on the MISTRA measured the amounts of time that members of the various twin pairs had spent together during their lives. This is illustrated in Figure 20, along the bottom. Note the 40-odd little circles in the diagram. Each one represents a twin pair in the MISTRA study. Their placement in the diagram describes their time spent together during their lives and their similarity on IQ tests. The further along the horizontal axis the circle is (i.e. the further to the right of the diagram), the longer was the time they shared together. The further up the vertical axis of the diagram they are, the more different are the members of the twin pairs in their IQs. Now, if there was an association between similarity of IQ and amount of time spent together during life we'd expect to see the circles, broadly speaking, arrange themselves along a line from the top left of the Figure (no time spent together and more difference in IQ) to the bottom right (more time spent together and less difference in IQ). Instead, what we see is a random-looking scatter of circles. There seems to be no association between the amount of time spent together and the similarity in the IQs. Do notice the range, though: one pair of genetically identical twins have an almost 30 IQ point difference; four other pairs cluster around the 18-point difference line. In some cases, then, there have been massive effects of the environment, but overall there is little evidence for this.

Let's get back to the details in Figures 15 to 18 and offer some numbers to indicate how intelligence gets passed on from generation to generation. Recall that the researchers in the field of behaviour genetics split the influences on our psychological make-up into three main sources: genes, environments shared with members of our family, and our individual or unique environmental experiences. The Minnesota studies that looked at separated twins reckoned that genes contributed about 70% to the influence on human intelligence differences and environment did the rest. Now, let's be clear what that means. It does not say that my or your intelligence score is 70% genetic. It means that, when we look at the *differences* in mental abilities across a range of adult people (twins, actually) in Western, developed countries, the *differences* between them in their mental capabilities are affected by genes to that degree. The Minnesota project is just one as yet incomplete study, not even a very large one, and it has still to report its full results. Looking across all the available studies in behaviour genetic research, one sees estimates of the genetic influence on intelligence differences that go from as low as 30% to as high as 80%. Rather conveniently, they average out to about 50%, meaning that about half the differences between people in their intelligence levels might be attributable to genetic differences.

None of the psychologists that I regularly talk to about intelligence differences cares much whether intelligence differences are attributable 40% or 70% to genetic differences. What we do know now is that intelligence differences have some appreciable genetic origins. What is much more interesting is to try to answer the following, more detailed

questions that result from knowing that *only some* of humans'
intelligence differences have their origins in the genes.

*Does the size of the influence of the genes change across the human
lifespan?*

Strangely, it appears that the influence of genes on intelligence grows
stronger as humans grow older. The proportion of intelligence
differences attributable to genes might be as low as 20-40% from
infancy to childhood, yet 60% or even quite a bit higher by the time we
get into our 70s and 80s. To me, this was originally counter-intuitive.
One's guess would be that as we accumulate education and knowledge
and insults to our brains from the environment over a long life then the
genes might have less and less effect. Not so. The first study to show the
very high genetic influence on intelligence test scores in old age was so
surprising that it made it to the top scientific journal *Science* and was
featured with pictures as a splash on their cover (Figure 21).

*What do we know about the influence of the environment on intelligence
test scores?*

We can see from the above numbers that the environment does indeed
have quite a large influence on human intelligence differences. If genes,
on average, account for about 50% of the differences between people in
intelligence, then the environment also accounts for about 50% of the
differences. Recall that the influences of the environment may be
partitioned into shared and unique effects – those we have in common
with our siblings and those that we experience alone. My guess and
yours, probably, would be that the lion's share of the environment's
influence would arise from the effect of the family. It's not so; by far the
larger part of the environment's influence can be traced to the non-
shared, unique environment. Families have little effect (when divorced
from the contribution of the genes). This is arguably the most shocking
result in the genetic/environmental study of intelligence. It was the

21. The cover page of the research journal *Science* for 6 June 1997, which reported the high level of genetic influence on intelligence differences in twins in late life.

topic dealt with by Judith Harris in her book *The Nurture Assumption* (i.e. the *incorrect* assumption that we all tend to make that upbringing is a big influence on intelligence level).

I think that this issue is crucial, and I also think that the way it is extracted from twin studies can be a bit abstruse, so I now want to introduce you to another remarkable study that suggests how limited an effect family upbringing has on intelligence.

Key dataset 8

Adoptees

Go to Figure 22, which is about adoption. I shall now describe a scenario and then ask some questions for you to think about before we look at the evidence.

- a mother (call her the 'birth mother') gives up her new-born baby for adoption
- the baby is adopted by another family (call them the 'adoptive mother and father'), who have their own child too
- the children grow up without the adopted child ever seeing the birth mother
- the birth and adoptive parents take intelligence tests and the

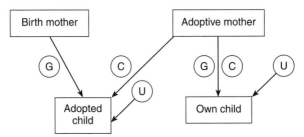

22. A diagram to show the influences on intelligence in adopted and natural children.

children take intelligence tests at different ages as they grow up

- remember, the adopted child spends all of his/her life with the adoptive parents and his/her step-siblings and none with the birth mother.

Now ask yourself:

1   Will the adopted child grow to have an intelligence level more like the adoptive mother and father, whom he/she has lived with from birth, or the birth mother, whom he/she has never met?
2   Since the step-siblings have spent their lives together in the same families, will they come to resemble each other in their intelligence test scores?

Anyone who believes there is an influence of family upbringing and environment on mental ability level is likely to predict that the adopted child will come to resemble the adopted mother and father and step-siblings in intelligence. Before unveiling the relevant findings, let me explain why such a prediction follows these beliefs.

Back to Figure 22 – and a reminder of the conventions that we used when we looked at twins. Examine the influences on the intelligence of the adopted child. His/her genes (G) come from the birth mother and father. (Here we are addressing only the birth mother's contributions.) The adopted person's 'common' family environment (C) comes from the adoptive mother (and father). The unshared/unique environment (U) is by definition not shared with anyone else and so is not really of interest here. Look at the 'own child' of the adoptive mother (and father). Both the genes (G) and the family environment (C) come from the same mother (and father). Therefore, we have two children who are genetically unrelated yet spend a lifetime in the same family. If there is an effect of family environment and upbringing on intelligence, then we expect to see step-siblings in the same family have some resemblance in their intelligence level. Also, if there is an effect of family environment on intelligence we expect to see some resemblance between the adoptive mother and her adopted child, perhaps greater than any resemblance between the birth mother and this adopted child, whom she never sees.

The test of these ideas came with the Texas Adoption Project conducted by John Loehlin and his fellow researchers. This project examined information from a church-based scheme in Texas in which mothers who were not married had offered up their children for adoption. Most of the birth mothers and adoptive mothers and fathers were white and middle-class. The children were adopted very soon after birth and were adopted on a permanent basis. The birth mothers and the adoptive mothers were given intelligence tests, including the Wechsler tests that we described earlier. The children were given intelligence tests at different stages: at an average of about 8 years and then an average of about 18 years.

Loehlin and his fellow researchers studied the data on intelligence test scores in several different ways to examine the effects of genes and the environment. The correlations between the intelligence test scores of the group of adoptive parents and their adopted children were around 0.1; these parent–children pairs share only environment and not genes. This suggests a very small effect of common family environment. Sometimes, more puzzlingly, the correlations between the group of adoptive mothers and their adoptive children were negative. That is, there was a slight tendency for more intelligent mothers to have less intelligent (adopted) children. This result would suggest that spending time together was making the adoptive children less (!) like their adoptive mothers in intelligence. The correlations between the intelligence scores of the group of adoptive parents and their own natural children were often around 0.2 or a bit more; these parent–child pairs share both genes and family environment. Thus, the parents with higher intelligence test scores tended to have natural children with higher intelligence test scores. This suggests an effect of genes adding to that of the common family environment in intelligence test scores. Most surprisingly, the highest correlations of all – often around 0.3 – were found between the group of adopted children and the birth mothers they had not lived with or even met after the first few days of life, which again points to the effects of the genes. Adopted children appear to grow more similar in intelligence level to a birth mother they have never met (with whom they share 50% of their genes) than to an adoptive mother with whom they spend their lives.

What happened when Loehlin and his colleagues compared pairs of siblings? Biologically related children in the adoptive families (i.e. children born from the same pairs of birth parents) have intelligence test scores that correlate about 0.3 or a bit less. But when biologically unrelated children who spend their lives in the same family are compared, then the correlations are around zero: they do not come to resemble each other in intelligence after a lifetime spent in the same family. Taken together, all these results suggest an effect of genes on intelligence and not much effect of family environment. Do recall the sizeable effect of unshared environment.

The other few adoption studies in this area are not huge, and the results are not definitive. However, when John Loehlin and two of his colleagues recently summarized their years of work with the Texas adoption project here was what they concluded:

> The results on IQ from the Texas Adoption Project are generally consistent with the results from other behavior-genetic methods, such as the comparison of identical and fraternal [non-identical] twins, or the study of twins reared apart. The major contributor to familial resemblance is the genes. Shared family environment has an appreciable effect when children are small, but this becomes minor by the time they are late adolescents. However, we found in our data some

tantalising suggestions that the full story of family effects may prove to be more complicated than this, in a weak *negative* environmental association between mothers' and childrens' IQs. A particularly striking manifestation was that the birth mothers showed, if anything, higher IQ correlations with the children they had had no contact with since near birth than the adoptive parents did with their own biological children with whom they had lived all their lives. (p. 123)

Do genes and the environment tend to affect general intelligence or the more specific cognitive abilities mentioned in Chapter 1?

Key dataset 9

We already know from Chapter 1 that there is general ability and there are identifiable, though related, specific types of mental ability, like verbal and spatial ability, memory, and mental speed. So, just as we asked about the effects of ageing on these different aspects in Chapter 2, we can now ask about the generality or specificity of the genetic effects.

I want to address this type of question using another remarkable dataset. It's the OctoTwin project in Sweden, featuring a group of identical and non-identical twins who have taken many intelligence tests. The remarkable thing is that they are all over 80 years old. In addition, they are relatively healthy and free from dementia. The project was following up previous studies that found that the genetic influence on specific mental abilities mostly came via genetic effects on general mental ability. That is, these previous studies found that: (1) general intelligence was quite strongly influenced by genes; (2) the group factors of ability were very strongly related to general ability; and (3) much of the differences among people in these group factors could be traced to the genetic effect on *general* mental ability. The OctoTwin project researchers wondered whether things were different as people grew much older.

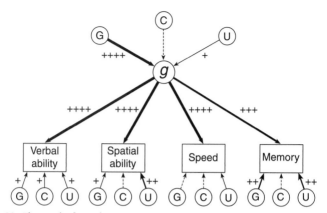

23. The results from the OctoTwin study, which show that differences in group factors of intelligence are heavily influenced by the genetic contribution to general intelligence.

Look at Figure 23. The picture of general mental ability – general intelligence *g* – and the special abilities or group factors that are related to it is familiar. Here we have used the special abilities that were measured by Stephen Petrill and his co-workers when they reported the OctoTwin results in the leading journal *Psychological Science*. In order not to have a Figure that was festooned with off-putting numbers, I have used the following labels: very strong associations have very thick black arrows and four plus signs; strong associations get three pluses; medium associations get two pluses and a thinner arrow; weak associations get a single plus; and where there is not much of an association at all there is a dotted line. You can see, then, that all of the four specific abilities are associated with a hypothetical general mental ability, or *g* factor; all of the arrows are very thick and have three or four pluses. Next I want to bring in the convention for looking at genetic and environmental (common and unshared) contributions to intelligence that were described in Figures 15–18 and 22. How much do genes and the environment contribute to the OctoTwin people's differences in general intelligence and to specific mental abilities?

Let's start with general intelligence – *g* – first. There is a very strong effect of genes on general ability. In fact, the results in this study indicated that, in people over 80, genes – G – contribute about 76% of the effects that result in intelligence differences. The other appreciable effect is from unshared environment – U. It contributes about 20% of the effects on individual differences in general ability test scores. Common environment – C – contributes almost nothing at this age.

So much for general ability. What about the specific abilities? Well, they are very strongly related to general ability. Take verbal ability as an example. Since it is so strongly related to *g* we see that the big genetic influence on *g* 'flows through' to verbal ability. That is, genes have a big effect on general ability at that age, and general ability contributes most of the differences in verbal ability, so the genetic effects that contribute to general intelligence differences play a big part in verbal ability differences. Therefore, the genetic influence on general ability contributes a lot to individual differences in all the more specific/group ability factors (stratum II in Chapter 1).

But *g* is not the full story with respect to the more specific abilities. It relates highly to them, but they are also independent of general ability to an extent as well. So, what affects the rest of the differences in group factors in mental ability? The answer lies at the bottom of the diagram. In addition to a *g* effect, each separable group factor (stratum II) in mental ability has genetic and environmental influences not shared with the other group factors and not due to *g*. Again, look at verbal ability as an example. There are additional, but weak, effects of genes and common and unshared environment on verbal ability that have nothing to do with general ability. For spatial ability there is a moderate additional effect of the unshared environment. Memory is the most interesting here. Note that it has two pluses leading from *g* to it. Therefore, as compared with the other three specific mental abilities, there is a greater proportion of the differences between people in memory to be accounted for that is *not* related to general mental ability.

Memory, over age 80 anyway, seems to be the ability that is least dependent on general intelligence. We see from the arrows at the bottom of the page that there are moderately strong influences of genes and unshared environment on memory differences that have nothing to do with the influences of genes and environment on general intelligence.

Do we know yet which genes have an influence on intelligence test score levels?

No. Researchers have discovered that genes play a sizeable part in influencing differences in mental ability between people, but as yet they have no idea what those genes are. By contrast with the case of some illnesses, they cannot point to a gene and say that if you have this form of the gene you will have such and such a level of ability. And the fact is that, outside the area of mental handicap, such a direct association between genes and intelligence is not going to happen. The best guess among researchers is that mental abilities are influenced by an unquantifiable number of genes, each of which will have a small effect. In the last few years the search for these genes that influence human mental ability levels has just begun. Only recently have laboratories begun to collect people's DNA and begun to ask which variants in DNA structure are associated with higher and lower levels of mental ability.

To follow this area up . . .

For general background on intelligence, genes, and environment, I found the following useful. Plomin's piece is written for a lay audience and includes more discussion of the social implications of genetic studies of intelligence

Bouchard, T. J. (1998). Genetic and environmental influences on adult intelligence and special mental abilities. *Human Biology*, 70, 257–79.
Plomin, R. (1999). Genetics and general cognitive ability. *Nature*, 402 (Suppl.), C25–C29.

Another good, and very straightforward and brief, article about intelligence, environment, and genes is the following.

Petrill, S. A. (1997). Molarity versus modularity of cognitive functioning? A behavioral genetic perspective. *Current Directions in Psychological Science*, 6, 96–9.

For a very clear description of the Minnesota twin study:

Bouchard, T. J., D. T. Lykken, M. McGue, N. L. Segal, & A. Tellegen (1990). Sources of human psychological differences: the Minnesota Study of Twins Reared Apart. *Science*, 250, 223–8.

Although the following book is aimed at the student and researcher, there are excellent descriptions of many key aspects of the genes and the environment and how they affect intelligence. See the chapter noted here for a good account of the Texas Adoption Project.

Loehlin, J. C., J. M. Horn & L. Willerman (1997). Heredity, environment, and IQ in the Texas Adoption Project. In R. J. Sternberg & E. Grigorenko (eds), *Intelligence, Heredity and Environment*. Cambridge: Cambridge University Press.

There were two good papers that I drew from in describing the Swedish study of old twins: both are technical, written for researchers.

McClearn, G. E. (et al.) (1997). Substantial genetic influence on cognitive abilities in twins 80 or more years old. *Science*, 276, 1560–3.
Petrill, S. A. (et al.) (1998). The genetic and environmental relationship between general and specific cognitive abilities in twins age 80 and older. *Psychological Science*, 9, 183–9.

There's a lot more to genetics and the environment and how they contribute to intelligence test scores than I have been able to introduce here. For more on important issues like 'gene–environment' interaction and correlation and the 'shared environment assumption' and so forth, see

Plomin, R. (et al.) (1997, 3rd edn). *Behavioral Genetics*. New York: W. H. Freeman.

If you are puzzled or annoyed at the apparent lack of influence of family upbringing on intelligence (and other psychological characteristics, too, it seems), you must read the following book, which is devoted to this finding.

Harris, J. R. (1998). *The Nurture Assumption: Why Children Turn Out the Way They Do*. London: Bloomsbury.

Chapter 5

The (b)right man for the job

Does intelligence matter?

Entire books – popular and scholarly – are available that disparage the invention and application of intelligence tests. It is certainly true that intelligence tests were used inappropriately and over-zealously at times during the 20th century, and to the exclusion of other important human characteristics. They are a tool that may be misused, to be sure. All tools run this risk, but, as Queen Elizabeth I ripostes in Sir Walter Scott's *Kenilworth*, ' "it is ill arguing against the use of anything from its abuse" ', so let us move on and ask if they have utility. And think what we are asking. It is this: does a score on a short test of mental ability have *any* predictive power for some aspects of real-life achievement? We are not asking whether an intelligence score *totally* predicts human achievements – it never does, or anything near it – just whether intelligence test scores have some useful predictive power.

The first tests of human intelligence appeared in 1905. They were developed by Alfred Binet and Theophile Simon in Paris. These two researchers were given a practical problem: how might the authorities identify those children who would not benefit from the normal style of education? The IQ-type tests, which now number many hundreds, were their answer. Therefore, what we call tests of intelligence were invented to serve a practical purpose.

Currently, the main applications of intelligence tests are in education, in the workplace, and in medicine. Thus, mental tests are used to assess mental capability in the settings of school performance, work performance, and in looking at the effects of illnesses and medical treatments on the brain's functions. It is well known that psychometric tests do a reasonable job of predicting educational attainment (see the Task Force report discussed in Chapter 7). There are other important factors too, but one's score on a mental test has some moderately strong relation to future educational achievements. However, for the illustration of the potential impact of mental testing I am going to focus on an application from the field of work.

Key dataset 10

The work-related dataset I shall refer to is a remarkable compilation of findings by John Hunter, with his research colleagues Ronda Hunter and Frank Schmidt. Their interests are in job selection, in finding the right people to do a job well. They asked the following simple-seeming question: is it worthwhile for an employer to select people for a job on the basis of, *among other things*, a test of general mental ability (general intelligence)? The emphasis here is not on each of the individuals offering themselves for selection: it is on those using the test to make the selection and it is centred on a practical problem. That is, imagine you are an employer and you wish to select people to begin new jobs in your workplace. What is the best method of selecting the most productive new staff? How can you tell who will bring the most benefit to your organization? In essence, among the criteria that you compile in your selection portfolio, would it be worthwhile having a test of general mental ability?

Before going that far, Hunter and his colleagues point out some factors that you as a hirer might wish to consider. First, is there any variability in people's performance on the jobs you are thinking about? If everyone does the job equally well, no matter what their personal qualities, strengths, and weaknesses, then why are you worrying about hiring decisions? If there is absolutely no difference in job performance between people then, with respect to productivity, you don't have a problem. (At least, not one to do with productivity; you might reasonably want to select people you'll enjoy working with.) That's unlikely: in most jobs there will be some people who do the job better than others. And the bigger these differences, the more you have to be concerned about whom you hire. If there are huge differences in how well people do the job for you, then you want to get the people who will do the job best.

The second factor with respect to hiring that Hunter talks about is the amount of selectivity you can apply in choosing. That is, do you have the luxury of taking those whom you consider to be the very best people for the job, or must you take whoever appears for the job interview? Imagine a situation where you have 10 jobs to fill and 100 people apply. That gives you the luxury of picking the top 10% of applicants, and if you have a good method of selection you can get the cream of that 100 into your business. What if only 20 people apply? Instead of getting the top 10%, you have to take the top 50%. You'll be selecting people who are not quite so good among the 10 successful applicants. If only 10 people apply you have to take all comers – those who will be good, mediocre, and poor at the job. Compared with the business that has the luxury of skimming off the cream, the top 10% of the best workers, you are going to lose productivity and income.

Help for aspiring employers there. But there is something missing so far. We've identified the fact that you only really need to worry about hiring decisions related to productivity when some people are better than others at the jobs you have vacant. Next, we've identified the fact that the more you are in a position to skim off the really best workers, the better are your chances of high production. The missing factor here is something that will identify the best workers. You need some basis for selection. You need some test that you can apply to your applicants so that you can pick out those people who will do the best job. You do not have infinite time or money to apply this test; the cheaper and quicker it is, the better. And, of course, the more accurately it can predict future job performance the better.

Does this really matter? Aren't we really discussing some small, marginal difference in income here? Perhaps we should worry less about productivity and focus more on giving everyone an equal chance of being hired, no matter what their qualities for the job. John Hunter provided some back-of-the-envelope calculations. He based his numbers on the USA's federal government around 1980. They hired about 460,000 people in any one year. The average tenure of their workers is $6\frac{1}{2}$ years. The average wage at that time was about $13,500. They were usually in the position of being able to select the top 10% of applicants; the jobs were popular and attracted many able people. Let's assume they have some method of selection that relates quite highly to job performance – a correlation of just over 0.5 between the selection 'test' and later job performance. (By the way, it is not easy to measure job performance, and it is often based upon ratings by supervisors in the studies we shall discuss.) Given this setting and these assumptions, Hunter worked out the difference in cost, based on productivity differences, between applying and not applying the selection 'test'. If you applied the selection 'test' in that situation, you would have a productivity gain of $15,610,000,000: over fifteen *billion* dollars (at 1980 prices).

In fact, that was Hunter's estimate of savings if you applied a simple test of general mental ability, a psychometric intelligence test, instead of nothing at all. What if you chose to interview the people rather than give them a psychometric intelligence test? You would lose $11,640,000,000 of the 15 billion dollars. You'd lose over 8 billion dollars of the 15 billion if you used only reference checks. Hunter concluded that not using a simple general mental ability test in hiring could cost up to about 20% of the USA's total federal budget in productivity losses. So, we might conclude that good hiring of the best potential workers can make a sizeable difference. Let's look at where Hunter got these figures.

Hunter and his colleagues have made a speciality of something called meta-analysis. What that means is that they tend not to do individual research studies themselves. Instead, they systematically search through the scientific literature for all of the research studies ever done on a topic and they try to put them together to come to a coherent, quantitative conclusion. The area that they meta-analysed is job-hiring decision-making. They have pored through studies conducted over 85 years of psychological research. They have read and filleted thousands of studies to form their conclusions. They have compiled a comprehensive guide to what is best in selecting for job performance. Though their research papers can be quite technical and bristling with statistics, they have a strong and simple message. Hiring decisions matter: they can make or lose you a lot of money. And there is nothing more important in hiring than having something, some set of open and fair criteria for selection, that relates as highly as possible to how well the person will do the job. That's the key then: what are the best ways of selecting people to do a job well?

In 1998 Hunter published a long paper with Frank Schmidt in the American Psychological Association's top review journal, the *Psychological Bulletin*. In it they examined the relative predictive power of 19 different ways of selecting people for jobs. Everything from interviews, through intelligence testing, and having people try out the job, to examining the applicants' handwriting (a popular method in France and Israel especially). There's a selected summary of these results in Figure 24; the diagram represents the cumulative knowledge from almost a century of research and thousands of research studies.

Look at Figure 24. Each of the columns represents a different way of hiring people (selection methods). The length of the column represents the size of the correlation between people's rankings on each selection

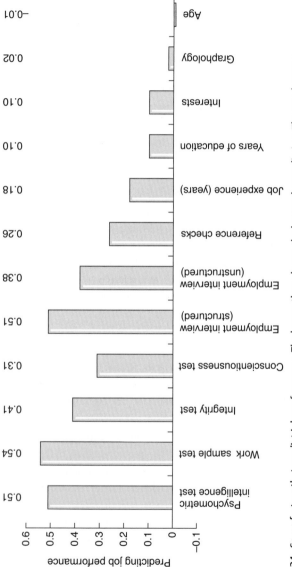

24. Some factors that predict job performance. The longer the column, the better the prediction. The numbers are correlation coefficients.

method and later performance on the job. The longer the column, the stronger is this relation. The longer the column, the better is the method of selection. The longest column belongs to work sample tests. This is the situation where you can get all of the applicants actually to do the job for a time and assess how efficient they are. These are costly to set up and they are far from universally applicable; by no means the majority of jobs lend themselves to this type of procedure. Note, too, that highly structured employment interviews do relatively well, but the more typical unstructured interviews are poorer. Reference checks on their own are not especially helpful. Years of job experience and years of education do not offer much information that's going to predict people's performance in doing the job. Age is totally uninformative and shouldn't be used as a selection criterion; and so is graphology, the analysis of handwriting. It tells you nothing about how well the person will do the job – and yet it is used widely in some countries for job selection. Not only is selection by this method losing people money in making sub-optimal selection decisions, the cost of having it done is wasted too. And it is unfair: it ends up rejecting people for something that is entirely unrelated to their ability to do the job.

In Figure 24 you can see that the column for the general intelligence/ psychometric test is comparatively long, almost as good as the best predictors of job performance. It does offer some useful information about how well people, on average, will do the job in many types of employment. Unlike other selection methods, it can be applied near-universally. It can be given for jobs where it is not possible to do a job tryout or compose a highly structured interview. For example, work sample tests can only be done by people who know how to do the job in the first place. Compared to most other methods, the general mental ability test is quick, cheap, and convenient. It has the lowest cost of any of the relatively good methods. Looking over the research literature, there is far, far more evidence for the success of the general mental ability test than any other method of selection. It's been used in many more research studies than any other method.

Tests of general intelligence have other merits in the job selection process. They are the best predictors of which employees will learn most as they progress on the job. They are the best predictors of who will benefit most from training programmes. However, the power of the general intelligence test to predict job success is not equal for all types of job. The more professional, the more mentally complex the job is, the more successfully the mental test score will predict the success on the job. Therefore, mental tests do poorest in totally unskilled jobs and are much better at predicting success on professional and skilled jobs. In their research report Schmidt and Hunter concluded that:

> Because of its special status, GMA [tests of general mental ability or general intelligence] can be considered the primary personnel measure for hiring decisions, and one can consider the remaining 18 as supplements to GMA measures.

What they meant was that you'd be well advised to use a test of general intelligence in most job-hiring situations, because they are cheap and quick and almost universally applicable, and modestly informative. But there's an obvious question that follows on from that. If we add some of the other hiring methods to a general mental ability test, which will add the most power to our hiring decisions? So Hunter looked at those methods which added the highest *extra* amounts of predictive power, assuming that we have *already* used a general intelligence test. The best was an integrity test, which added another 27% to the predictive power. Giving a work sample or a structured interview would both add 24% extra predictive power. Where these could be applied then, it would be sensible to add one or more of these to the general mental test. Using multiple methods is sensible in these cases, because it leads to even better decisions. Tests of conscientiousness and reference checks are also helpful additions to the general mental ability test.

In this setting then – finding a bunch of people who will do a range of jobs better than just taking people at random – an intelligence test has utility. No, it will not predict all that strongly how well people do a job. Yes, you will still hire people who are hopeless and with whom you can't get on. But, on the whole, you'd be better off including a general mental ability test in your portfolio of selection methods.

In order to avoid an accusation of gross over-simplification, let me repeat that we all know it takes more than brains to be successful, and sometimes it does not take brains much at all. Returning to Sir Walter Scott's *Kenilworth*, we can see that the young Walter Raleigh, as he addressed some older and less successful courtiers, knew that he could progress far beyond them, given the possession of other qualities.

> 'Why, sirs,' answered the youth [Raleigh], 'ye are like goodly land, which bears no crop because it is not quickened by manure; but I have that rising spirit in me which will make my poor faculties labour to keep pace with it. My ambition will keep my brain at work, I warrant thee.'

work

To follow this area up . . .

These papers are technical along the way, but the discursive sections are written with laudable clarity. These authors make their forceful conclusions lucidly, having first assembled frighteningly large bodies of evidence. If the latter paper were not so new I should have no hesitation in calling these papers 'classic' works in psychology.

Hunter, J. E. & R. F. Hunter (1984). Validity and utility of alternative predictors of job performance. *Psychological Bulletin*, 96, 72–98.
Schmidt, F. L. & J. E. Hunter (1998). The validity and utility of selection methods in personnel psychology: practical and theoretical implications of 85 years of research findings. *Psychological Bulletin*, 124, 262–74.

More applications of intelligence testing in education and the workplace are summarized in the American Psychological Association's Task Force report that is covered in Chapter 7. I strongly recommend you read that. If you are interested in the origins of the first mental tests by Binet in France and their subsequent export to (and over-use in) the USA, then the most comprehensive and fair book I have read on this topic is the following.

Zenderland, L. (1998). *Measuring Minds: Henry Herbert Goddard and the Origins of American Intelligence Testing*. Cambridge: Cambridge University Press.

For details of research papers my colleagues and I have produced over the last 15 years or so, visit my website at *http://129.215.50.40/Staff/staff/ijd/pubs_complete.html*. A substantial proportion of these research reports used mental ability tests in medical settings, to discover whether some medical conditions and some medical treatments damage or enhance human intelligence test scores. That type of research is nowhere gathered together as a single body; it was not possible to describe it in the setting of a meta-analysis in the way that I was able to do because of the Hunters' research in job selection.

As an example of how mental ability tests play a leading role in some medical issues, here's an editorial article I wrote with a colleague in 1996 for the *British Medical Journal*. This is also available on the *British Medical Journal* website, which has free access: (*http://www.bmj.com/cgi/content/full/313/7060/767*).

Deary, I. J. & B. M. Frier (1996). Severe hypoglycaemia in diabetes: Do repeated episodes cause cognitive decrements? *British Medical Journal*, *313*, 767–8.

So far in this chapter I have emphasized the practical uses of intelligence tests for the users of the tests: the business person who wants to hire the best staff, the doctor who wants to know about her patients' mental capacities, and so forth. Another angle on the utility of tests is to ask what they mean to you: that is, what are the betting odds on life outcomes given a certain level of intelligence? Linda Gottfredson's chapter explains that intelligence tests are not testing abstruse, academic abilities, and that they relate to important outcomes across the whole range of life's domains. *The Bell Curve* (discussed in more detail in Chapter 7) is also worth a look.

Gottfredson, L. (2000). *g*: Highly general and highly practical. In R. J. Sternberg & E. L. Grigorenko (eds), *The General Intelligence Factor: How General Is It?* New York: Lawrence Erlbaum.
Herrnstein, R. J. & C. Murray (1994). *The Bell Curve*. New York: Free Press.

work

Chapter 6
The lands of the rising IQ

Is intelligence increasing generation after generation?

If my score on an IQ-type test is higher than yours, then does it mean that I am brighter/cleverer than you? If the test used was one of the best indicators of the general intelligence factor, or if it was one of the more comprehensive test batteries, such as one of the Wechsler tests, then we might be persuaded provisionally to accept that conclusion and ask for more information. We might be further persuaded if we were genetically related and lived in a similar culture. The next dataset calls the mental ability testing enterprise into question by demonstrating large differences in mental test scores *in just those situations where we might expect similarity*. The key researcher involved is James Flynn, a political scientist working at the University of Otago, New Zealand. He has provided researchers in the field of human intelligence with a scientific conundrum and massive communal headache.

The first thing Flynn brought to serious scientific scrutiny was that mental test companies had to renorm their scores every so often. This rather boring-sounding, technical problem was the source of one of the largest unexplained puzzles in the field of intelligence research today. When you buy a mental test from a psychometric company, you get the test questions and the answers, and you get instructions for giving the test in a standard way so that everyone who takes the test gets an equal chance to score well on it. But, imagine that you have now tested someone on the test: you will realize that you need something else. The person's score does not mean anything unless you have some indication of what is a bad, good, and indifferent score. Thus, with the test, when you buy it, you will get a booklet of normative scores, or 'norms'. This is a series of tables which indicate how any given score fits into the population's scores. Usually they are divided for age, because some test scores change with age (Chapter 2). Therefore, you can find out how your testee did when compared with their age peers. Usually the tables with tell you what percentage of the population would have scored better and worse than the score that your testee obtained. Those of us with children and who measured their heights and compared them with the population average for their ages will be familiar with this type of referencing.

James Flynn noticed that these tables of norms had to be changed every several years. As new generations came along they were scoring too well on the tests. The tests seemed to be getting easier. A generation or two after the companies produced the tables of normative scores, the 'average' person of the later generation was scoring way above the 'average' person of the earlier generation. For example, 20-somethings tested in the 1980s were doing better on the same test than 20-somethings from the 1950s. The norms were becoming outdated – 'obsolete' was Flynn's term. (There's an ironic parallel with the trend in A-level results in England. Children have been scoring better than they used to on these tests, with resulting arguments about whether the teaching is better or the examinations are getting easier. At least, in the case of IQ-type tests, the content has remained the same.)

The response of the test companies was to 'renorm' the tests. The norms tables were altered so that, as time went on, it became harder to achieve a score that got you above any given percentage of your peers. Thus, if you scored *the exact same test score on the exact same test* in, say, 1950 and 1970, you would have a higher IQ in 1950 than in 1970. In fact, it can be seen as worse than that. Let's say you take the test on the last day that the institution testing you used the old norms. You take the test and you obtain a given score. The tester looks up the norms tables and states that you make the cut above some percentage of your age peers. If you took the same test on the first day of the new norms the same score would put you significantly further down the percentage of the population. In fact, the test companies would not always alter the norms tables. The other manoeuvre they adopted was to make the test harder so that you had to take a new, harder test to get to the same point on the population scale.

In summary, as the 20th century progressed, the whole population's scores on some well-known mental tests were improving when compared with same-age people generations earlier. Just as average height has increased over generations, people began to wonder if intelligence was rising.

Flynn published a scientific paper in *Psychological Bulletin* in 1984 that gave IQ test-users an alarm call to a potential disaster. 'Everyone knew' that tests had to be renormed every so often, but Flynn quantified the effect and spelled out its consequences. He quantified the effect in a smart piece of psychological detective work. He searched for every study he could find in which groups of people were given two different IQ tests for which the norms were collected at least 6 years apart. This is the key idea. Flynn set about asking: what would the sample's estimated IQs be when compared with the earlier and the later norms? For clarity, he decided to look exclusively at samples of white Americans. He found 73 studies, involving a total of 7,500 people, aged from 2 to 48 years. These studies involved the Stanford–Binet and the Wechsler scales, tests at the very centre of the intelligence testing world.

Flynn found that subjects' estimated IQs were higher when they were compared with older norms, by contrast with more recent ones. On perusing all the samples involved, it became clear that the effect was fairly constant over the period from 1932 to 1978. During that time white Americans gained over 0.3 of an IQ point every year, about 14 IQ points over the epoch. So, over the middle part of the 20th century, the American IQ rose by a massive amount. Flynn warned us:

> If two Stanford–Binet or Wechlser tests were normed at different times, the later test can easily be 5 or 10 points more difficult than the earlier, and any researcher who has assumed the tests were of equivalent difficulty will have gone astray. (p. 39)

> Allowing for obsolescence in intelligence testing is just as essential as allowing for inflation in economic analysis. (p. 44)

This takes some reckoning with and becomes even more surprising when the trend in SAT scores is added to the picture. The Scholastic Aptitude Test (SAT) is a high-level test taken at the end of school by America's educational elite. It is well documented that, over the period in which IQ scores were rising, the verbal scores – call it general knowledge for now – on the SAT were declining. And SAT scores and IQ scores are very highly correlated: yet one is decreasing over time while the other increases. If the IQ increases over time reflect a real rise in intelligence, and the SAT decreases are real decrements in knowledge, then one is forced to conclude that that aspect of the SAT that does not depend on intelligence (remember, IQ and SAT are highly correlated) must have gone down. Something that determines SAT scores (but not intelligence level) must have suffered massively at the same time that IQ went up. As Flynn worried:

> But it is precisely at this point that one's head begins to spin: do less demanding textbooks and low-level TV programs raise intelligence while lowering verbal skills; do declining standards in schools sharpen the mind while undermining study habits; does student absenteeism mean students are engaged in mentally demanding tasks while missing out on knowledge; does a demoralised family environment boost IQ while lowering motivation? (p. 38)

Perhaps, though, it's not as bad as that. It could just be that the test companies are not testing appropriately representative groups of people in their attempts at making up their norms. They might be going out generation after generation and getting it wrong by testing ever-more biased, more clever samples for their norms tables, making it harder for those being tested to do well by comparison. Or perhaps the contents of the tests are steadily leaking out over time to the public so that people in successive generations have had more experience with the items? Thus, at the end of his first large-scale study, James Flynn came up with three points that might explain the 'massive gains' that successive American generations were attaining in IQ scores.

1 *Artefact*. The gains might be 'not real, but an artefact of sampling error'. That is, the groups recruited to provide norms might, over time, become more biased toward containing cleverer people. This is very unlikely to have occurred in such a systematic way as to make all later normative samples brighter than all earlier ones. But even if this is the explanation, it still makes scores across IQ tests non-comparable.

2 *Test sophistication*. Successive generations might not actually be more intelligent; they might just be scoring better on the tests for some reason that we have to go and find. This leaves us the large, additional problem of explaining the reason for SAT test scores declining.

3 *A real intelligence increase*. If the test score differences represent real increases in intelligence, they are very hard to explain. Flynn tried to examine the most likely candidate: that socio-economic improvements accounted for the IQ gains across generations. However, the gargantuan alterations that would be needed in living standards to account for the IQ changes were just not plausible.

James Flynn wanted more definitively to identify the source of the rising IQ scores. Broadening out from the USA, he sought examples of IQ test scores that had been collected across generations. Here's how he described that search:

> The method used to collect data can be simply put. Questionnaires, letters, or personal appeals (usually a combination of all three) were sent to all those researchers known to be interested in IQ trends on the basis of scholarly correspondence and the exchange of publications. One-hundred sixty-five scholars from 35 countries were contacted. They came from Europe (every nation except Albania, Denmark, Greece, and Portugal); Asia (Japan, India, and Israel); Latin America (Argentina, Brazil, Chile, Cuba, Mexico, and Venezuela); the Caribbean (Barbados and the U.S. Virgin Islands); and the Commonwealth (Australia, Canada, and New Zealand). American data were available from a previous study. Military authorities in charge of psychological testing were contacted in every European country, plus Australia, Canada, Greenland, Iceland, and New Zealand, as were 21 educational research institutes in Western Europe and the Commonwealth. (p. 171)

Key dataset 11

This is typical of James Flynn. He does nothing by halves, and he has thrown over 20 years of his academic life into scouring the world for data to address the 'rising IQ' problem. Some of Flynn's strongest data came from military samples, in those countries where nearly all young men were given IQ tests at entry to compulsory military service. Figure 25 illustrates some of Flynn's data.

Here's how to look at Figure 25. The vertical scale at the left-hand side is an IQ scale. Along the horizontal are some different countries from which Flynn got good data. In each country the most recently available data have been set at an arbitrary IQ score of 100. These appear at the top of the 5 vertical lines. An IQ of 100 is, by an arbitrary definition, the population average. For each of the 5 countries in the Figure there were earlier testings of the same population. The dates down the dotted

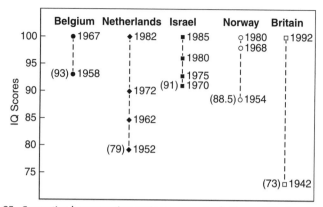

25. Generation by generation, nations are scoring better on IQ tests.

vertical lines shows just how much lower the populations' IQs were in earlier testings. Note the dots on each vertical line with a date against them: these dates are when the IQ testings of the population took place. If you read across from these dots/dates to the left you can see what the average IQ of the population was at that date, compared with the 100 score of the most recently tested population. Please note that we should expect that all of these testings would give rise to average IQs of 100. They do not. Whenever a population was tested at an earlier date the imputed IQ average was lower. The effect found among American whites was also found in many other countries, leading Flynn to name his 1987 *Psychological Bulletin* article 'Massive IQ gains in 14 nations'.

Take the example of the Netherlands. Since 1945 the Dutch military have tested almost all young men in the Netherlands on 40 of the 60 items of Raven's Progressive Matrices. This is a non-verbal mental ability test and is supposed to be quite good at testing general intelligence. Flynn examined these data and reported the percentage of young men who were scoring more than 24 of the 40 items correct. The percentages were:

31.2% in 1952
46.4% in 1962
63.2% in 1972
82.2% in 1981/2.

Setting the 1982 scores to a mean IQ of 100, one can work back and ask the question: what was the mean IQ score of the earlier generations based on the percentage that achieved the pass rates? Figure 25 reveals that the Dutch men in 1972 averaged around IQ 90, the 1962 population around 85, and the 1952 population below 80. Additional proof of this increase arose from a comparison of over 2,800 men tested in 1981/2 and their fathers tested in 1954. The sons were 18 IQ points higher than their fathers who had been tested $27\frac{1}{2}$ years earlier. Thus, as I hinted in the first paragraph of this chapter, we see this puzzling effect in people who are genetically related and who have lived in the same culture, where we would expect similar average IQ scores.

Look again at Figure 25. Norwegian data for approximately the same period show gains for later generations too, but they are smaller than those of the Dutch. Belgian military data showed a rise of 7 IQ points over the relatively short period from 1958 to 1967. New Zealand children gained an average of 7.7 IQ points between 1936 and 1968 (data not shown). Two further sets of data from Flynn's large number of comparisons are shown: Israelis gained 11 IQ points over the 15 years from 1970 to 1985 and people in the United Kingdom went from a putative mean IQ of 73 in 1942 to 100 in 1992.

This last increase makes a good illustration of the impact if these changes were real alterations in intelligence levels. Compared with a mean of 100 in 1992, the mean for the population in 1942 would be almost at a level that indicated mental handicap for the *average* person. (It is this consideration that makes me very sceptical about the veracity of these supposed 'IQ gains'.) In the end, Flynn found reasonable data on 14 nations and for a generation (30 years) he found IQ gains between

5 and 25 points, with an average of 15. These data are stunning, and very challenging for researchers in the field of intelligence.

One key fact to focus on when thinking about the 'Flynn effect' of rising IQ scores is that the biggest effects tend to occur in so-called culturally reduced tests. That is, the rises occur most markedly in those tests that do not seem to have contents that can easily be learned. For example, Raven's Progressive Matrices is among the tests that show the highest gains. Yet Raven's Matrices involves finding the correct answer that completes an abstract pattern. It has no words, no numbers, nothing really that can be taught so that the later generation will do better than the former. Flynn's review of his massive datasets confirmed this.

> A consensus about the significance of generational IQ gains depends, therefore, on whether they manifest themselves on culturally reduced tests like the Raven's. These tests maximise problem-solving and minimise the need for more specific skills and familiarity with words and symbols. [There are] strong data for massive gains on culturally reduced tests: Belgium, the Netherlands, Norway, and Edmonton show gains ranging from 7 to 20 points over periods from 9 to 30 years; when the rates of gain are multiplied by 30 years, they suggest that the current generation has gained 12–24 points on this kind of test. Tentative data from other nations are in full agreement. This settles the question at issue: IQ gains since 1950 reflect a massive increase in problem-solving ability and not merely an increased body of learned content. (p. 185)

The Flynn effect is well established. Its importance is reflected in the eponymous title, and in the interest it has attracted since the late 1980s. The American Psychological Association had a full meeting on the issue, and published a book in which many experts sought an answer to it. It is easy, and accurate, to summarize by saying that experts are dumbfounded. There are two broad responses to the Flynn effect.

The first response is to suggest that the Flynn effect is real, marking an actual improvement in brain power in successive generations across this century. People who opt for this account suggest that we have a good exemplar in height. Human height has increased across the century as a result of better nutrition and general health, so why not intelligence? Flynn himself seemed not to favour this option. He worked out that, in countries such as the Netherlands and France, where there have been high IQ gains across generations, teachers should now be faced with classes in which 25% are gifted and where geniuses have increased 60-fold! 'The result should be a cultural renaissance too great to be overlooked.' (p. 187) Flynn searched French and Dutch newspapers, especially periodicals relating to education, from the late 1960s to the present and found no mention of any great increase in intellectual achievements by newer generations.

The second response suggests that the Flynn effect is an artefact. It is not the case that people are more intelligent. Instead, what has happened is that people have become more familiar with the test materials. Children's toys, magazines, television programmes, computer games, and so forth might contain materials that have IQ-item-like properties, and so people do better on the tests when they come across them. This might be termed the 'Early Learning Centre' theory.

There is one thing to note about the Flynn effect that Flynn himself has been keen to emphasize. Though the effect is clearly important, it does not compromise the validity of mental test scores *within* generations. Mental test scores, despite the 'massive gains' through time, do retain their reliability, their ability to predict educational and job successes, and their heritability, but only *within* each generation. The key point is that something in the environment (many researchers believe that it has to be the environment because some of the across-generation samples tested fathers and sons) of many countries across the middle years of the 20th century has led to ability scores increasing substantially.

Flynn makes a telling point when he asks us to reflect on the fact that being born a generation or so apart can make a difference of 15 IQ points. We have no good account of the causes for this change; it is officially mysterious. Given, though, that he could find no evidence for the present generation's genius in achievement over former generations, Flynn says that IQ tests like Raven's do not measure intelligence, but only some correlate of intelligence, which he calls 'abstract problem-solving ability'. Further, he insists that differences in this ability are 15 points between successive generations, and these differences must arise from some environmental factor. He concludes that IQ test differences cannot be used to make trustworthy comparisons of the intelligence of different generations or of different cultural groups.

The reader might like to reflect on the Flynn effect and its causes, not least because some fresh thinking on this matter might offer psychologists a foothold on a slippery problem. If there was a prize to be offered in the field of human intelligence research, it would be for the person who can explain the 'Flynn effect' of the 'rising IQ'.

To follow this area up. . .

James Flynn's oeuvre consists of three rather stunning research papers. The last of these is the most accessible, giving a general, popular summary of his findings. The second half of it is about Flynn's view of social justice and how intelligence differences fit into that view: it's intelligent, humane, and worth looking at.

Flynn, J. R. (1984). The mean IQ of Americans: Massive gains 1932 to 1978. *Psychological Bulletin*, 95, 29–51.

Flynn, J. R. (1987). Massive IQ gains in 14 nations: What IQ tests really measure. *Psychological Bulletin*, 95, 29–51.

Flynn, J. R. (1999). Searching for justice: the discovery of IQ gains over time. *American Psychologist*, 54, 5-20.

The former two papers are full of details about datasets from around the world. Had they been written by a psychologist I feel sure they would be as dry as dust. Flynn, probably because of his background, makes the accounts readable, and he tries to spell out even the technical stuff so that one need not be a psychometrician to understand them.

The American Psychological Association's book which addresses the continuing conundrum of the Flynn effect contains a good range of opinion: from those who think there has been a real rise in IQ in recent decades (usually citing better nutrition as the key factor) to those who think the Flynn effect is an artefact (more educational toys and TV programmes, etc.) or something more complex. What I can tell you is that this book assembled an impressive list of relevant international researchers and none has a convincing explanation of the 'rising IQ'.

Neisser, U. (ed.) (1998). *The Rising Curve*. Washington, DC: American Psychological Association.

increasing IQ

Chapter 7

Eleven ~~Twelve~~ (not-so-) angry men (and women)

Psychologists actually agree about human intelligence differences

A key working party

As an interested layperson, it can't be easy or satisfying trying to get to grips with some straight facts about human intelligence differences. The highly visible experts in the area tend to represent one extreme or the other in advocating IQ-type testing. Media coverage reflects this, tending to put one side of the debate, or just the two extremes, or merely reporting the slanging match. Many years ago a proponent and antagonist of human intelligence testing, Hans Eysenck and Leon Kamin respectively, jointly wrote a book about intelligence. Its title was *The Battle for the Mind*. They wrote separate sections on the research as they saw it, and they responded to each other's sections. The result was heat rather than enlightenment for the reader. The writers were further apart at the end than they were at the start. What hope is there for the general, curious reader when the cognoscenti are inhabitants of this Babel?

In fact, it took a big furore to knock some heads together and for psychologists to come to a clear realization that there *was* a strong consensus about the research findings on human intelligence, right across the spectrum of researchers. The result was one of the most

AMERICAN PSYCHOLOGIST

IQ:Knowns
and
Unknowns

Fall River Revisited

David Foley

Journal of the American Psychological Association   February 1996 Volume 51 Number 2 ISSN 0003-066X

26. The cover page of the *American Psychologist* for February 1996, which featured the American Psychological Association's Task Force report 'Intelligence: knowns and unknowns'.

useful accounts of intelligence research ever to become available for the non-specialist.

The furore: in the mid-1990s a book called *The Bell Curve* rewrote the rules for academic book distribution. Close on 900 pages long, almost 300 of which were statistical analyses, detailed footnotes, and academic journal references, it sold in the USA in the hundreds of thousands. It brought just about every dispute concerning IQ freshly to the pages of newspapers and magazines, and got the Western world (at least) and the psychological research community in a turmoil over the impact that mental ability has on our destinies. It excoriated the body of intelligence research by addressing IQ scores in the context of social outcomes and social policy. The resulting tintinnabulation from the chattering classes alerted the professional psychological associations: if people were arguing about IQ, shouldn't they at least have some undisputed facts as a basis for commenting on *The Bell Curve's* contents?

The response: the American Psychological Association (APA), the largest and most authoritative professional psychological society in the world, became fed up with uninformed argument on intelligence. Not prepared any longer to stand on the sidelines, they decided they had a responsibility to put on record the findings about human intelligence that attracted very wide consensus among psychologists. Their Board of Scientific Affairs (BSA) appointed a Task Force to collect together what researchers did and did not know about human intelligence differences. My aim in this chapter is to show that the report from this Task Force is the best available, unbiased summary of the topic. It will add variations to the themes raised in this book and is a good first source of further reading.

The Task Force's report comprehensively and concisely tells the wider world what is and is not known about human intelligence (IQ) differences. Here's how they introduced their report:

In the fall of 1994, the publication of Herrnstein and Murray's book *The Bell Curve* sparked a new round of debate about the meaning of intelligence test scores and the nature of intelligence. The debate was characterised by strong assertions as well as strong feelings. Unfortunately, those assertions often revealed serious misunderstandings of what has (and has not) been demonstrated by scientific research in this field. Although a great deal is now known, the issues remain complex and in many cases still unresolved. Another unfortunate aspect of the debate was that many participants made little effort to distinguish scientific issues from political ones. Research findings were often assessed not so much on their merits or their scientific standing as on their supposed political implications. In such a climate, individuals who wish to make their own judgements find it hard to know what to believe.

Ulric Neisser, Professor of Psychology at Emory University, was appointed chair. Other members were chosen by an extended consultative process, with the aim of representing a broad range of expertise and opinion, and included nominees from the APA Board on the Advancement of Psychology in the Public Interest, the Committee on Psychological Tests and Assessment and the Council of Representatives. Disputes were resolved by discussion. As a result, the report had the unanimous support of the entire Task Force.

It is difficult to overestimate the importance of this Task Force for wider communication about the study and understanding of human intelligence differences. Ulric Neisser is one of the best-known research psychologists in the world, the father of 'cognitive psychology', the area of psychology that studies mental processes. Much respected, he had not previously been associated with mental testing and was clearly both disinterested and authoritative. On the panel itself was a range of experts one might have expected to argue vigorously and acrimoniously rather than to agree. There were well-known researchers from the field of the genetic–environmental studies of intelligence

(Thomas Bouchard and John Loehlin – their work was featured in Chapter 4), and from the more exclusively environmental approach (Stephen Ceci). There were people who took a broader view of intelligence: for example, Nathan Brody, who had dispassionately summarized the area of intelligence difference for fellow academics; and Robert Sternberg, whose theories of intelligence differences go far beyond the typical conceptions of mental ability as encapsulated in IQ tests. There were representatives from the USA's Educational Testing Service (Gwyneth Boodoo) and people with an interest in the education of minority groups (A. Wade Boykin), in differences between the sexes (Diane Halpern), and in testing as applied to occupational outcomes (Robert Perloff). This was the world's largest and most influential psychological association knocking some very respected and disparately opinioned heads together and mandating them to come up with a clear, unanimous statement about the knowns and unknowns of human intelligence differences.

There follows a guide to the contents of the Task Force's report: I have indicated where it picks up issues raised in this book.

Concepts of intelligence

The first topic the Task Force addressed was the key question of what psychologists mean when they study intelligence. They agreed that the word covered many aspects of mental working and their relative efficiency but that

> When two dozen prominent theorists were recently asked to define intelligence, they gave two dozen somewhat different definitions ... Such disagreements are not cause for dismay. Scientific research rarely begins with fully agreed definitions, though it may lead to them.

They did recognize that the main conception of intelligence differences was encapsulated in the so-called psychometric approach. Psychometric means measurement applied to aspects of the mind, and this is the field that tends to be associated with the idea of intelligence testing. As we saw in Chapter 1, tests of mental measurement cover a wide range of mental abilities. In addition, though, the Task Force recognized the part played by conceptions of intelligence that emphasize aspects of mental ability that are not covered by typical IQ-type tests. To repeat, what is tested by mental ability (intelligence) tests is by no means all that human brains are capable of. The Task Force report discusses a wide range of conceptions of intelligence that attempt to go beyond an IQ-type view of mental abilities.

Intelligence tests and their correlates

This next section of the Task Force's report asked whether mental test scores relate to anything else. A scientist may measure some aspect of mental functioning and find that some people score better than others: however, in all honesty he cannot claim that the test scores derive from some prior definition of intelligence. Unlike height or blood pressure, there is no scale from zero to whatever. The measurements of mental ability are not reflecting known aspects of the body's functioning. The cognitive tasks involved in the intelligence tests might be demonstrably mental, but why should one be interested in them? For three reasons, perhaps.

First, if the test scores are substantially stable through our lives, then some partly consistent aspect of our mental ability has been reckoned. This was covered in my Chapter 2, and the Task Force report usefully summarizes other research in this area.

Second, if the tests' scores can usefully help to predict some aspects of human life that are independent of the test materials, then they have significance that is wider than the surface content. The areas of life in which the tests are applied are work, school, and clinic. These issues are often to do with the tests' capacity to act as a convenient aid to selection and prediction. The Task Force report discussed in some detail the associations between intelligence test scores and school performance, years of education, job performance, and broader social outcomes such as crime and delinquency. Some aspects of these – mainly selection in the workplace – were described in Chapter 5 of this book.

Third, there is another aspect of correlates of intelligence test scores to do with where the differences in scores come from. That is, can we discover anything about the brain's performance that relates to mental test score differences? If this were possible, and if some of the differences in mental test scores were related to aspects of brain processing, then we would be in a better position to understand how the differences in brains produce differences in mental ability. The Task Force's report discusses how intelligence test scores correlate with components of cognition, reaction time, inspection time, and aspects of neurological function. In Chapter 3 of this book some of these supposedly simpler aspects of brain function that relate to mental test scores were introduced.

The genes and environment and intelligence

The APA Task Force's report considered the evidence for genetic and environmental contributions to differences between people in their mental abilities. Their report goes into more detail and covers more individual studies and topics than was possible in this book (Chapter 4). With regard to the environment, the Task Force agreed that one of the most intriguing findings to emerge in recent years is the generation-upon-generation rise in IQ test scores (discussed here in Chapter 6).

Group differences in intelligence

The last topic which the APA's Task Force addressed was group differences in intelligence. These 'groups' were based upon the sexes and ethnic groups. I have not dealt with these topics in the present book and I recommend the Task Force's treatment of these at times controversial issues.

I end this summary of the Task Force's report by listing some of the critical factors that its members believed remain unanswered or mysterious about human intelligence, despite almost a century of research. Here, according to the Task Force's report, are some of intelligence researchers' unknowns, some challenges for future research.

- There is some influence of genes on intelligence, but its exact nature is unknown.
- The aspects of the environment that affect intelligence are unknown.
- It is not clear how nutrition affects intelligence.
- It is not known why intelligence test scores correlate with simpler measures of human performance (see Chapter 3 of this book for examples of these 'simpler' measures).
- There is no satisfactory explanation of why intelligence test scores are increasing with successive generations.
- The reasons for intelligence test score differences between various groups are not known.
- There is too little known about the important human abilities that are not tested by intelligence tests (creativity, wisdom, practical sense, social sensitivity).

To follow this area up. . .

I can't repeat enough that this piece is a must if you want to know more about human intelligence. It is even-handed, well-informed, wide-ranging, and easy to read. This is very definitely the next thing to read on human intelligence.

Neisser, U. (et al.) (1996). Intelligence: knowns and unknowns. *American Psychologist*, 51, 77–101.

Further reading

I hope this Very Short Introduction has stimulated your interest in human intelligence differences. If you want to go further, this section provides some general guidelines. More detail on sources and suggestions for further reading by topic appeared at the end of each chapter in the book.

Resources on the internet
The best place to start is the excellent report called 'Intelligence: knowns and unknowns' by the American Psychological Association's Task Force. This is comprehensive, concise, non-technical, and disinterested and tackles controversial topics in a way that is open and sensible. The American Psychological Association's own summary of this report is available on the world wide web at *http://www.apa.org/ releases/intell.html* and the entire report is available free at *http:// www.lrainc.com/swtaboo/taboos/apa_01.html*. You can also contact the APA's public office for a copy of the report.

Another very good summary of the field of research on human intelligence differences was a special issue of the magazine *Scientific American Presents*. The Winter 1998 edition (volume 9, number 4) was called 'exploring intelligence' and had accessible articles on intelligence testing, multiple intelligences, general intelligence, the *Bell Curve* study, gifted children, the evolution of intelligence, and animal intelligence.

There's a free copy of Linda Gottfredson's article on general intelligence and its importance on the internet at *http://www.sciam.com/ specialissues/1198intelligence/1198gottfred.html*. Gottfredson is an able, strong, and persuasive advocate of general intelligence and its practical importance and impact. Her article nicely broadens the work of Hunter that we saw in Chapter 5.

If you feel you would like some sort of 'reaction' to the intelligence orthodoxies I have served up here, I feel a duty to point you toward some intelligence dissenters and sceptics. In the interests of balance, then, Howard Gardner gives a thoughtful account of some key recent issues in intelligence – whether there is more than one type of intelligence, whether intelligence is heritable, and whether emotional intelligence is a valid idea – in an article in the *Atlantic Monthly* in February 1999, entitled 'Who owns intelligence?'. He's the psychologist who wrote the popular *Multiple Intelligences*. He takes the view that there's a lot more to intelligence than that which is measured by the sorts of tests I have focused on. You can find it at *http:// www.theatlantic.com/issues/99feb/intel.html*.

General searches on the internet by title of work or author may lead you to other interesting sites. One further site which I can recommend has many articles on intelligence (history, testing, applications, beyond intelligence). It's at *http://www.sccu.edu/ psychology/webintelligence.html*.

Printed resources

1 Sources for the general reader

First, I have not laid a great deal of emphasis on introducing what mental test items look like, and I have not knocked up a quick-and-dirty IQ test for this book. If you want more detail on what a test might look like, there are loads of cheap, IQ self-testing books. I should not lay great store on the scores they give or the rank that they put you in. However, at least they offer an inkling of the sorts of mental work some intelligence tests demand. Eysenck (1990) is the one I would recommend.

Eamon Butler & Masden Pirie. (1983) *Test Your IQ*. London: Pan.
Hans J. Eysenck. (1990). *Know Your Own IQ*. Harmondsworth: Penguin.
Hans J. Eysenck. (1994). *Test Your IQ*. London: Thorsons.
Ken Russell & Phillip Carter. (1999). *Test Your IQ*. London: Foulsham.

Most general books on intelligence decry rather than defend the study and applications of intelligence tests. I must be frank: I do not agree with much of the opinion expressed in the three books that follow, but all are well written and make some interesting points. You might as well know the range of opinion that this area of research attracts and you could not do better in getting the critical voice than to read one or more of these.

Stephen J. Gould. (1997, 2nd edn). *The Mismeasure of Man*. Harmondsworth: Penguin.

reading

This is almost entirely critical of the idea of intelligence testing, especially the notion of general intelligence. It's an odd book, because it has sold very well despite having quite a lot of technical information, about the history of intelligence testing and the statistics involved in mental measurement: it is superbly written. Note that the sections on brain size are out of date and he has refused to correct this despite being sent newly available published data by researchers. People in my research field have severely criticized his account of the statistics of mental measurement. A flawed book, but a great read.

Michael Howe. (1997). *IQ in Question*. London: Sage Publications.

This is an entirely critical account of testing intelligence, genetics and intelligence, applications of intelligence, and group differences in intelligence. Short, clearly written, but a very one-sided book.

Ken Richardson. (1999). *The Making of Intelligence*. London: Weidenfeld and Nicolson.

This energetically points out the flaws in intelligence testing and especially decries studies on the genetics of intelligence, suggesting that intelligence testing should be banned because it is a social evil. Again, this is a one-sided account that makes no disingenuous efforts at 'balance'.

We can't ignore the elephant sitting in the corner, and if you want to be a credible commentator on intelligence's recent family row it's worth having a look at *The Bell Curve*.

Richard J. Herrnstein & Charles Murray. (1996). *The Bell Curve*. New York: Free Press.

Oddly for a book with hundreds of pages of technical, statistical information and calculations, it is extremely easy to understand. The book is a strange mixture. In part it is a thesis about the emergence of a cognitive elite in American society and the danger of a social apartheid based on cognitive ability differences. In part it is a series of analyses of the predictive power of IQ and social class on some of life's outcomes. The authors certainly wrote some of the clearest accounts of statistical analyses I have ever read, and they communicated widely, selling over half a million copies in the USA. However, the book has spawned volumes and volumes of critical books and articles, amounting to what has been called 'The Bell Curve Wars'. Just search the internet using the search term 'Bell Curve' and you'll see what I mean.

2 Sources intended for students

Colin Cooper. (1999). *Intelligence and Abilities*. London: Routledge.

Readable and up to date, Cooper's book deals with a similar range of topics to that covered in this book, sometimes focusing on different datasets. It has more statistics, and if you want to get more of a handle on the technical issues, this is quite a good, though still selective, introduction.

N. J. Mackintosh. (1998). *IQ and Human Intelligence*. Oxford: Oxford University Press.

A heavyweight, comprehensive account of the topic from the Professor of Psychology at Cambridge University, this book does assume some basic knowledge of statistics, but it is readable and has a stentorian, at times wry and dyspeptic, 'voice' commenting on research on intelligence. This is one book used with my students. If you want to get something that is detailed, covers the whole area, and is well written, this is the best book.

Arthur R. Jensen. (1998). *The g Factor*. London: Praeger.

Long, technical, comprehensive, and definitely a book that is on the side of the intelligence tester, this massively well-documented treatise on why general mental ability exists and is important is the book you must visit if you want to know why Gould, Howe, and Richardson (see above) get so worked up.

Robert J. Sternberg (ed.). (2000). *Handbook of Intelligence*. Cambridge: Cambridge University Press.

This is a near-700-page book, covering most aspects of intelligence. Each chapter is written by an acknowledged expert in the area. I have to declare an interest and say that I wrote one of the chapters (on intelligence and simple information processing). The book's sections are: the nature of intelligence and its measurement; development of intelligence; group analyses of intelligence; biology of intelligence; intelligence and information processing; kinds of intelligence; testing and teaching intelligence; intelligence, society and culture; intelligence in relation to allied constructs. This is another key book used with my students.

If you want to get into the general area of the genetic and environmental contributions to human intelligence and other aspects of human psychology, the best book on the market is the following. The authors bend over backwards to make technical material comprehensible.

Plomin, R. (et al.) (2001, 4th edn). *Behavioral Genetics*. New York: W. H. Freeman.

3 Sources for researchers

There are many monograph and edited books on the topic of intelligence. These are highly specialized and the likelihood is that so few people would follow them up that none is worth mentioning here (I mentioned one of my own at the end of Chapter 3). It might, though, be interesting for readers to know that the key academic journal that deals with matters related to intelligence is called *Intelligence*, published by Elsevier. The journal's editorial office is at the Department of Psychology in Case Western Reserve University in Cleveland, Ohio, USA. This is the principal location for researchers to communicate new research findings.

Index

Intelligence

Intelligence

Expand your collection of
VERY SHORT INTRODUCTIONS

Visit the
VERY SHORT
INTRODUCTIONS
Web site

www.oup.co.uk/vsi

➤ **Information** about all published titles

➤ News of **forthcoming books**

➤ **Extracts** from the books, including titles not yet published

➤ **Reviews** and views

➤ **Links** to other **web sites** and main OUP web page

➤ Information about **VSIs in translation**

➤ **Contact** the editors

➤ **Order** other **VSIs** on-line

PSYCHOLOGY
A Very Short Introduction
Gillian Butler and Freda McManus

Psychology: A Very Short Introduction provides an up-to-date overview of the main areas of psychology, translating complex psychological matters, such as perception, into readable topics so as to make psychology accessible for newcomers to the subject. The authors use everyday examples as well as research findings to foster curiosity about how and why the mind works in the way it does, and why we behave in the ways we do. This book explains why knowing about psychology is important and relevant to the modern world.

'a very readable, stimulating, and well-written introduction to psychology which combines factual information with a welcome honesty about the current limits of knowledge. It brings alive the fascination and appeal of psychology, its significance and implications, and its inherent challenges.'

Anthony Clare

'This excellent text provides a succinct account of how modern psychologists approach the study of the mind and human behaviour. ... the best available introduction to the subject.'

Anthony Storr

www.oup.co.uk/vsi/psychology

Also by Ian Deary

Looking Down on Human Intelligence
From psychometrics to the brain

What is it about human brains that make some people more capable than others? In an authoritative and critical account, Professor Ian Deary reviews historical, cognitive, and biological research on the foundations of human mental ability. Where most previous accounts of intelligence have examined how human mental ability can predict success in education, work, and social life, few books have taken as a starting point mental ability (and individual differences in intelligence), and attempted to see what factors could have influenced, and even predicted mental ability. New to the highly acclaimed Oxford Psychology Series, *Looking Down on Human Intelligence* reveals what we know about the origins of intelligence.